Flavors of Africa
Cookbook

Books by Dave DeWitt, Mary Jane Wilan, and Melissa T. Stock

Hot & Spicy & Meatless

Hot & Spicy Chili

Hot & Spicy Latin Dishes

Hot & Spicy Southeast Asian Dishes

Hot & Spicy Caribbean

Hot & Spicy Mexican

Hot & Spicy & Meatless 2

Flavors of Africa Cookbook

Spicy African Cooking—From Indigenous Recipes to Those Influenced by Asian and European Settlers

Dave DeWitt
Mary Jane Wilan
Melissa T. Stock

Illustrations by Lois Bergthold

Prima Publishing

Library of Congress Cataloging-in-Publication Data

DeWitt, Dave.
  Flavors of Africa: spicy African cooking—from indigenous recipes to those influenced by Asian and European settlers / Dave DeWitt, Mary Jane Wilan, Melissa T. Stock : illustrations by Lois Bergthold.
    p.   cm.
  Includes index.
  ISBN 0-7615-0520-2
  1. Cookery, Africa.   I. Wilan, Mary Jane.   II. Stock, Melissa T.   III. Title.
TX725.A4D48   1997
641.596—dc21   97-26084
                                                                     CIP

98 99 00 AA 10 9 8 7 6 5 4 3 2 1

Printed in the United States of America

How to Order
Single copies may be ordered from Prima Publishing, P.O. Box 1260BK, Rocklin, CA 95677; telephone (916) 632-4400. Quantity discounts are also available. On your letterhead, include information concerning the intended use of the books and the number of books you wish to purchase.

Visit us online at http://www.primapublishing.com

Contents

Acknowledgments

Thanks to the following people who helped to make this book possible: Michelle Cox, Arlen Greene, Susan Hunter, Tsuma Nzole Kalu, Nancy and Jeff Gerlach, Rosemary Ann Ogilvie, Judith Ritter, Denice Skrepcinski, Richard Sterling, D. Michael Warren, and Nick Zehnder.

Introduction

Despite its size and the diversity of its countries, the continent of Africa is a culinary mystery to most North American cooks. Perhaps the most familiar African dishes come from North Africa. However, they are not as chile-infused as ones from other regions.

The great news for chile cooks is that African chiles are easily duplicated by most of the varieties commonly available in North America—and to an ever-increasing extent, the United Kingdom and Europe. So we've simplified the cooking process by recommending the most familiar available chiles for those described in tribal dialects. We've provided as much information as we could collect on that subject in our Glossary of African Food and Cooking Terms (p. 247).

We attempted to collect as many authentic African names of the chiles and recipes as we could. But since more than 2,000 languages are spoken on the continent, we found that most of the recipe titles were in English or Swahili. When we know a tribal or regional name of a recipe, we have listed it after the English title.

This book would not be complete without the help of our correspondents who either live in or traveled to Africa. They are mentioned in our Acknowledgments, but we'd like to single out a few people who were particularly helpful. Nick Zehnder of the Johannesburg Book Store specializes in cookbooks, and he was very helpful in providing African volumes that were unavailable in North America. Michelle Cox of the Driftwood Beach Club in Malindi, Kenya, was particularly helpful in teaching us about Kenyan cuisine. And our good friend Richard Sterling provided invaluable assistance through his trips to Egypt and East Africa. For West Africa, we relied heavily on information from D. Michael Warren, a professor of anthropology at Iowa State University and an honorary chief of the Yoruba of Ara, Nigeria.

A note on the Heat Scale: We've used the same Mild, Medium, Hot, and Extremely Hot ratings as in our Hot & Spicy cookbook series. They are based on our own tastes, taking into consideration the type of chile in the recipe, the amount used, and its dilution with other ingredients. Cooks who wish to increase or decrease heat levels based on these ratings can easily adjust the amount of chile.

Unusual chiles and other ingredients can be obtained from our Mail-Order Sources (p. 255).

Chiles in Hottest Africa

The exciting cuisine of Africa reflects the diversity of its fifty-four countries, which span a vast area; the nation of Sudan alone is larger than the United States east of the Mississippi River. This exotic, inspiring land is marked by topography ranging from lush rain forests to snowy mountain tops, and its climates include both the arid and the tropical.

The cooking of the African continent reflects the influences of its explorers, its conquerors, and its traders. Chiles were unknown in Africa before 1500, but they conquered a continent in less than half a century. The Africans embraced the imported New World Capsicums with a fervor unmatched except, perhaps, by the people of India and Mexico. As African food expert Laurens van der Post observed, "The person who has once acquired a taste in the tropics for African chiles becomes an addict."

African Nomenclature and Tolerated Weeds

There are dozens, if not hundreds, of names for the pungent pods of Africa. The Portuguese there call the chile *pimento*, the English refer to it as *chilli*, the Muslim words for it are *shatta* and *felfel*, and the French word for chile is *piment*. The Swahili words for chile are *pili-pili*, *piri-piri*, and *peri-peri*, which are regional variations referring to both chiles and dishes made with particularly pungent pods. The differences in spelling result from different tribal pronunciations of "L" or "R." Tribal names vary greatly: Chile is *mano* in Liberia, *barkono* in northern Nigeria, *ata* in southern Nigeria, *sakaipilo* in Madagascar, *pujei* in Sierra Leone, *foronto* in Senegal, and the ominous *fatalii* in the Central African Republic.

In much of Africa today, chiles are tolerated weeds. Birds deposit the seeds in peanut or cotton fields, and the plants that sprout are cultivated by the farmers only in the sense that they do not chop them down. The chiles become associated with the cotton or peanut crops and thrive from the maintenance of those fields. The chile plants are perennial, and they ripen year-round in the tropical regions. They are expensive to handpick, yet have become an important wild-harvested crop in some regions. In some countries, as we shall see, chiles are an important cultivated commercial crop.

Spice-Laden North Africa

Since the Arabic countries north of the Sahara are linked culturally, economically, and gastronomically more closely with the Mediterranean region

2

than with the rest of Africa, there is little doubt that chiles first appeared in North Africa. In the first place, the Strait of Gibraltar separates the Iberian Peninsula and North Africa by only a few miles, so it is a logical assumption that chiles would filter southward from Cadiz to Tangier by at least the early 1500s. In the second place, the Turks completed their conquest of North Africa in 1556 and, since they had already introduced chiles into Hungary, it makes sense that they also carried them to Tunisia, Algeria, and Libya.

The first chiles to appear in North Africa were probably small, extremely hot *annuums*, closely related to cayennes, which were and still are mostly used as dried red pods or ground into powders. Morocco and Tunisia are the largest producers of chiles in North Africa, followed by Sudan, which sells its chiles to Egypt. By cooking with the chile recipes that exist today, we can taste dishes that are centuries old because the cuisines of North Africa have hardly changed at all.

A complex and powerful spice compound is the chile-based *harissa*, of Tunisian origin but found all over North Africa. *Harissa* (p. 22) is a paste featuring red chiles for heat and color and curry spices such as cinnamon, coriander, and cumin for flavor. It is used in the kitchen and at the table to fire up soups, stews, and less spicy curries, so it is at the same time a condiment, a marinade, a basting sauce, and a salad dressing. *Harissa* is often served on the side as a dipping sauce for grilled meats, such as kebabs, and is also served with couscous.

The most famous North African chile dishes, served from Morocco to Egypt, are called *tajines,* and they are named after the earthenware *tajine* pot in which they are cooked. Just about any meat—chicken, pigeon, mutton, beef, goat, and even camel—can be made into a *tajine.* (Because of Muslim beliefs, pork is never used.) The meat in a *tajine* is usually cubed, and, according to Harva Hachten: "The cooking liquid is the secret of a *tajine*'s tastiness. This is usually a combination of water, butter or oil (characteristically, olive oil), and seasonings to suit what's being cooked."

A *tajine* is cooked for a long time to allow the ingredients to become very tender and the cooking liquid to reduce to a thick, savory sauce. *Tajines* have varying consistencies and can either be stews or casseroles. Our recipes appear in the soups and stews, meats, and poultry chapters (Chapters 4, 5, and 6).

In Morocco, couscous is king—a "national dish." As kings are likely to do, it has invaded the rest of North Africa also. In most servings, it not only has its own chiles, but is "married" to *harissa* sauce; they are inseparable.

The name of the dish is onomatopoeic, meaning that it emulates the sound the steam makes as the grains of semolina cook.

African Bird Peppers

Although chiles probably appeared first in North Africa, they probably did not spread into the rest of Africa from that region. It is more likely that chiles were introduced farther south into Africa by Portuguese explorers and traders. Even before Columbus, Portuguese exploration of Africa had proceeded down the west coast of the continent between 1460 and 1488. When Vasco da Gama rounded the Cape of Good Hope, crossed the Indian Ocean, and landed in India in 1498, he established the trade route for spices and other goods that the Portuguese controlled for over a century.

By 1482, the Portuguese had settled the western "Gold Coast" of Africa, and by 1505 they had colonized Mozambique on the east coast. By 1510, they had seized Goa in India and had established a colony there. During this time, it is suspected that chile peppers were introduced by way of trade routes between Lisbon and the New World. By 1508, Portuguese colonization of the Pernambuco region of Brazil meant that both the *annuum* and *chinense* chiles prevalent there were made available for importation into Africa. The introduction of sugar cane into Brazil in the 1530s and the need for cheap labor was a cause of the trade in slaves, and an active passage of trade goods between Brazil and Africa sprang up.

The most likely scenario for the introduction and spread of chile peppers into Africa south of the Sahara is as follows. Varieties of *Capsicum annuum* and *chinense* were introduced into all West and East African Portuguese ports during the forty years between 1493 and 1533, with the introduction into West Africa logically preceding that of East Africa. The chiles were first grown in small garden plots in coastal towns by the Portuguese settlers and later by the Africans. Although it is has been suggested that chiles were spread throughout Africa by Europeans during their search for new slaves, the simplest theory is the more likely one.

The Portuguese may have been responsible for the introduction of chiles into Africa, but spreading them was for the birds. History—and evolution—repeated themselves. In precisely the same manner that prehistoric chiles spread north from South to Central America, chiles conquered Africa.

African birds fell in love with chile peppers. Attracted to the brightly colored pods, many species of African birds raided the small garden plots and then flew farther inland, spreading the seeds and returning the chiles to the wild. Chiles thus became what botanists call a *subspontaneous crop*—newly established outside of their usual habitat, and only involuntarily spread by humans.

From West Africa, birds moved the peppers steadily east, and at some time chiles either reached the coast of East Africa or met the advance of bird-spread chiles from Mozambique and Mombasa. The birds also spread chiles south to the Cape of Good Hope. We must remember that these chiles were being spread by birds centuries before the interior of Africa was explored by Europeans. So when the early explorers encountered chiles, it was only natural for them to consider the pods to be native to Africa.

West Africa: Magic and Medicine

The German explorer G. Schweinfurth reported that the natives of West Africa concocted a magic potion from wild chiles that ensured eternal youth. Other explorers observed that chiles were used to spice up dried locusts, which were considered a tasty snack in some parts of Africa. In 1871, when the American Henry Stanley finally found the "lost" David Livingstone, he discovered that the Scottish explorer had lived on meat and gravy seasoned with wild chiles. Livingstone also told him that the native women sometimes bathed in water spiced with chile powder in order to increase their attractiveness.

Pierre de Schlippe, a senior research officer at the Yambio Experimental Station in the Congo, reported in 1956 that chiles had become the most important cash crop after cotton in the Zande district; they required, as he put it, "very little encouragement and no supervision whatsoever." He wrote, "It is safe to assume that chiles as a cash crop had no influence on agricultural practice whatever."

During the early days of chile production in Nigeria, chiles were grown in patches near houses and as field crops under the shade of locust bean trees. They were planted in late May, and the chiles were ripe and ready for picking by November. One source reported that soon after Nigerian farmers began planting chiles, they were getting a four- to eight-thousand-pound yield per acre and, as early as 1938, were exporting 100 tons a year.

Today, Nigeria and Sierra Leone are major producers of many varieties, including the moderately pungent *funtua* chile. In Nigeria, approximately 150,000 acres of all varieties of chiles are under cultivation; it is the largest producer of chiles in Africa, accounting for about fifty percent of all production. Most of the chile is consumed domestically, although some is exported to the United Kingdom.

As might be expected, the food of Nigeria is distinguished by an extra infusion of hot chiles. As Ellen Wilson, author of *A West African Cookbook,* has observed: "Learning to eat West African food means learning to enjoy [chile] pepper." She added: "West African dishes can be searing or simply warm, but it is noticeable that the [chile] pepper never conceals the other ingredients; in fact, it seems to enhance them."

Curries are particularly popular in Nigeria, and one of their distinguishing characteristics is that they are served with an inordinate number of accompaniments. In addition to the usual chutneys, raisins, and shredded coconuts, the Nigerians offer as many as twenty-five condiments, including chopped dates, diced cucumber, diced citrus fruits, ground dried shrimp, diced mangoes and papayas, peanuts, grapes, fried onions, chopped fresh red chiles, and bananas.

"Nigerians and old African hands," noted Harva Hachten, "spoon out a portion of everything so their plates become a mound of curry and rice completely hidden by a patchwork of color and tastes."

Approximately ninety-one percent of the agricultural households in Liberia grow hot peppers, as most of the main dishes of the country contain them. Fresh peppers are marketed, but the pods are also ground into powders and made into hot pepper sauce. Most of the varieties grown are local cultivars, but the jalapeño and *yatasufusa,* a Japanese variety, are also grown. There is no export of chiles from Liberia, as the entire crop is consumed locally.

In addition to their heavy application in foods, chiles have medicinal uses in West Africa. Fresh green and red pods are eaten whole as a cold remedy, undoubtedly to clear out the sinus cavities. In 1956, L. Stevenel, a French Army officer, noted an interesting medicinal usage of chiles in Africa. Writing in *The Bulletin of the Society of Exotic Pathology,* Stevenel attributed the absence of varicose veins and hemorrhoids in the natives to the constant use of red chile in their diet. "Native workers on the railroad always carry a supply with them and consider them as a panacea necessary for good health," he wrote. Stevenel claimed that he had cured his own hemorrhoid problem and that of his fellow officers by adding red chile pulp to their food. The cure worked quickly—in a matter of days—but only with red chiles; green chiles were ineffective. Although Stevenel did not state why red chiles worked and green did not, we suspect the reason could be connected with the high concentration of vitamin A in red chiles.

East Africa: *Piri-Piri* and *Berbere*

Historically, East Africa gained importance in the spice world as the principal source of extremely pungent peppers known generically as Mombasa chiles, named after the principal port in Kenya from which they were shipped. However, the chiles came not only from Kenya, but also from Uganda, Tanzania, and Malawi. The chiles were both cultivated and collected in the wild, and they were varieties of the *piquin* pod type, which ranged from the spherical "bird's-eye" chiles to elongated pods an inch or more in length.

Reputedly, the hottest African chiles are those called Mombasa and Uganda, which are *Capsicum chinense,* probably introduced by the Portuguese from Brazil. In some parts of Africa, these habanero-type chiles are called "crazy-mad" peppers, and, reputedly, they were reintroduced into the Caribbean islands during the slave trade.

Chiles in many East African countries are cultivated on plantations amidst banana trees, and a chile export industry began in Uganda in the early 1930s. Uganda was the biggest producer and exporter during the first half of the twentieth century, but production dwindled to practically nothing by the mid-1970s, and the slack was taken up by the islands of Zanzibar and Pemba.

During the same period of time in Kenya, Europeans as well as Africans took to the chiles so much that local consumption caused exports to drop dramatically. Thus it is not surprising to learn that East African foods are as heavily spiced with chiles as are the West African dishes. Kenyans serve a stew called *kima,* which combines chopped beef with red chile powder and curry spices. It is obviously derived from the *keema,* or mincemeat curries, of India. East African cooking has been greatly influenced by Indian curries, which are usually not prepared powders but rather combinations of chiles and curry spices that are custom-mixed for each particular dish. Tanzanians are fond of combining goat or chicken with curried stews, or simply charcoal-broiling the meats after they have been marinated in a mixture of curry spices and chiles.

7

One of the most famous East African dishes is *piri-piri,* Mozambique's "national dish." The same word describes small, hot, dried red chiles; a sauce or marinade made with those chiles; and the recipes combining shrimp, chicken, or fish with the *piri-piri* sauces. Such fiery combinations are so popular in Beira and Maputo that *piri-piri* parties are organized. The dish has even been introduced into Lisbon, where it is served with less chile heat.

Another large East African producer of chiles is Ethiopia, but most of the chiles are used domestically in their highly spiced cuisine. The varieties most commonly grown are "Bakolocal" and "Marekofana," both known generically as *berbere,* which is the same name as the spice paste made from them. The average daily consumption of chiles in Ethiopia is a little more than half an ounce per person, so they are as much a food as a spice. The main reason for this is their inclusion in local curry-like dishes.

Ethiopia is the part of East Africa least influenced by British and Indian versions of curry. Instead, they evolved their own unique curry tradition. According to Daniel Jote Mesfin, author of *Exotic Ethiopian Cooking,* "Marco Polo did not visit our country. And Ethiopia was never conquered. It came under brief Italian rule during Mussolini's time, but for the most part, we did not have direct and intimate dealings with foreign powers. And Ethiopian cuisine remained a secret."

Ethiopia was isolated from Europe, but not from the spice trade. "Since Ethiopia was located at the crossroads of the spice trade," observed Michael Winn, owner of New York's Blue Nile restaurant, "its people began to pay keen attention to blending spices. Fenugreek, cumin, red chiles, and varieties of herbs are used lovingly in creating meat, fish, and vegetable dishes."

The most important spice mixture is a condiment called *berbere,* which is made with the hottest chiles available—the "Bakolocal" and "Marekofana," as mentioned previously—plus other spices. *Berbere* is served as a side dish with meat, used as a coating for drying meats, or used as a major ingredient of curried meats. Tribal custom dictated that *berbere* be served with *kitfo,* a raw meat dish that is served warm. According to legend, the more delicious a woman's *berbere* was, the better chance she had to win a husband. Recipes for *berbere* were closely guarded, as the marriageability of women was at stake.

Laurens van der Post philosophized on *berbere* in 1970: "*Berbere* gave me my first inkling of the essential role played by spices in the more complex forms of Ethiopian cooking. . . . It seemed to me related to that of India and

8

of Indonesia, particularly Java; I suspect that there may have been far more contact between Ethiopia and the Far East than the history books indicate." Chile peppers are obviously extremely important in Ethiopian curries, and they have even inspired a derogatory expression, *ye wend alich'a,* meaning "a man who has no pepper in him."

In Ethiopian cookery, *berbere* is an indispensable ingredient in the "national dishes" known as *wa't,* or *we't* (depending on the transliteration), which are spicy, curry-like stews of lamb, beef, chicken, beans, or vegetables (never pork).

South Africa: A Concentration of Curries

"There is reason to assume that the ambrosia of which the ancient poets spoke so often was a kind of ginger chile called *pinang* curry," wrote C.L. Leiopoldt, the Afrikaans poet. Chile-laced curries are extremely popular in South Africa because of a unique collision of culinary cultures.

The Dutch colonized South Africa because of its ideal position halfway between the Netherlands and the Spice Islands. It was a perfect outpost for raising the vegetables and livestock necessary to replenish their ships. In 1652, the Dutch East India Company dispatched a party of officials to the Cape to establish a "revictualling station."

"Within fourteen days of their arrival," wrote Renata Coetzee in *The South African Culinary Tradition,* "these early settlers had laid out a vegetable garden." They planted sweet potatoes, pineapples, watermelons, pumpkins, cucumbers, radishes, and citrus trees such as lemons and oranges.

Late in the seventeenth century, with the "revictualling station" in operation, commerce between the Dutch East India Company and the new Dutch colony of South Africa picked up considerably because of an important commodity: Malay slaves, referred to in South African literature as "the king of slaves." The men were utilized as farmers, carpenters, musicians, tailors, and fishermen, while the women were expert cooks who not only introduced exotic Spice Islands dishes, but also imported the spices necessary to prepare them.

Among the Malaysian spices transferred by the slaves to South Africa were aniseed, fennel, turmeric, ginger, cardamom, cumin, coriander, mustard seed, tamarind, and garlic. Chiles, of course, were introduced by both birds and the Portuguese traders, and eventually were disseminated across

South Africa. Curiously, coconuts—so important in the Spice Islands—do not play a role in South African curries.

The Cape Malays, as the slaves' descendants were called, developed a unique cuisine called "Old Cape Cookery." It evolved into a mixture of Dutch, English, and Malay styles and ingredients, with an emphasis on the Malay. Predominant among the numerous cooking styles were curries and their accompaniments. As early as 1740, "kerrie-kerrie" dishes were mentioned in South African literature. That terminology had changed by 1797, when Johanna Duminy of the Riviersonderend Valley, wrote in her diary: "When the evening fell I had the candles lit, the children were given their supper and put to bed. At nine o'clock we are going to have a delicious curry."

Johanna's curry probably was milder than that of today in South Africa, because for a time chiles and green ginger were greatly reduced for the Dutch palate. But the Cape Malays relished the heat, and Harva Hachten, author of *Kitchen Safari,* pointed out: "Curries are as much a part of Malay cooking as they are of Indian."

A Note on the Chiles Recommended in This Book

Most African varieties of chiles, such as *pili-pili,* are not available in North America, but fortunately their counterparts are. Therefore, we have specified the common North American varieties that most closely match their African cousins. Cooks should stock red and green New Mexican chiles, cayenne, *piquins,* habaneros, and jalapeños.

From Zahtar to Berbere: *Spice Mixtures and Condiments*

We begin with the basic recipes that are essential to African cookery and will be used in later recipes. There are a myriad of African condiments that contain chiles. We had to exercise some restraint to keep this chapter from being twice its size. We were particularly surprised by the number of Ethiopian sauces, pastes, and spice mixtures, so we have included a few of those.

Curries are enormously popular in Africa, but most cooks prepare their own spice mixtures rather than spending the money on imported curry powders from India. Of all the curry powders we ran across in our research, Malawi Curry Powder (p. 14) was our favorite, probably because it was hotter than the curry powders from South Africa.

In North Africa, spice mixtures are popular for flavoring the *tagines,* or stews, that abound there. We found one mixture, *ras al hanout,* that contains twenty to thirty ingredients, including belladonna berries and Spanish fly—those notorious cantharides beetles. We have opted for two less controversial mixtures: *Zahtar* (p. 16), with flavors of sesame and cayenne, and *Tabil* (p. 17), a Tunisian favorite combining coriander, caraway, and garlic, which is used on grilled meats.

Ethiopian cooks flavor their stews (*we't*) with mixtures such as *We't* Spices (p. 18), with its unusual blending of cloves and turmeric. More powerful is Very Hot Ethiopian Spices (*Mit'mit'a,* p. 19), which fires up raw meat dishes called *kitfo.* Such dishes are similar to those served in Lebanon and are much tastier than you might imagine.

Cape Malay *Sambal* (p. 20), a spice and chili mixture from South Africa, shows the influence of the Cape Malays, immigrants from Malaysia who brought their own ingredients and cooking styles to Africa. Other South Africans loved the cuisine and adopted it, and its popularity is similar to that of Indonesian food in The Netherlands. This *sambal* adds heat to virtually any South African meal.

Few people are aware that Madagascar, an island nation off the coast of Mozambique in East Africa, has its own tradition of highly spiced foods. Madagascar Sauce Dynamite (p. 21) is not only a condiment, it can be used as a marinade or baste for grilled meats, poultry, or even fish.

From North Africa comes one of the more famous African condiments, *Harissa* Sauce (p. 22), which is a popular addition to *tajines* and couscous dishes. Another sauce from the same region is Berber Barbecue Sauce (p. 24), with its unique combination of raisins, curry powder, peanuts, and honey.

Although similarly named, *Berbere* Paste (p. 25) is unrelated to Berber Barbecue Sauce, as it is from a different region with a different language. The paste is used both as a condiment and a cooking ingredient. A similar condiment is Ethiopian Green Chile Paste (*T'iqur Qarya Awaze,* p. 26), which is used as dip for grilled meats.

The next four sauces hail from West Africa. A classic is West African *Pili-Pili* Sauce (p. 28), utilizing the generic *pili-pili* pepper, which has an amazing number of incarnations. Most of them resemble small cayenne chiles, but since the word means "pepper-pepper," nearly any chile can be substituted.

The word "sauce" also has a number of connotations in West Africa; sometimes, as with *Palaver* Sauce (p. 30), it means "stew" as much as "sauce," and can be a meal when served over rice. Sauce *Gombo* (p. 31) is thickened with okra (*gombo*), which is also the thickening agent in gumbo, a stew that was transferred to the southern United States from Africa by slaves. Sauce *Gombo* is served over vegetables or starchy foods, such as potatoes and plantains, while the classic Nigerian Fried Red Pepper Sauce (*Ata Dindin,* p. 32) is usually served with meats.

We jump from West to East Africa for our next four sauces. Tsuma Nzole Kalu's Special Sauce (p. 34) is a Kenyan sauce for grilled or roasted meats, especially game, while Ugandan Groundnut Sauce (p. 35) is generally served with fried foods such as chicken or fish. Sauces with peanuts are very popular in both East and West Africa. Pumpkin Hot Sauce (*Yedubba We't,* p. 36) and Ethiopian Curried Butter (*Nit'ir Quibe,* p. 37) are two unusual sauces again from Ethiopia. The former is used over starchy foods, while the latter can be a spread or dip for *injera,* a bread made from buckwheat, or any other type of bread.

We close out our Condiments chapter with two favorites from South Africa that are served with curries: Yellow Peach Pickle (p. 38) and Cape Town Apple-Raisin Chutney (p. 39). The South Africans love their fruits and regularly use them in spicy condiments.

MALAWI CURRY POWDER

This blend is the hottest curry powder we found in Africa, although some pastes like *berbere* might top it on the heat scale. To make it milder, while retaining its chile flavor, substitute one dried red New Mexican chile for the *piquins*. In Malawi, the spices are traditionally sun-dried before being ground, and are not toasted. Note the large number of cloves in this recipe, possibly the result of influence from nearby Madagascar, a clove-growing island.

10 small, hot, dried red chiles, such as *piquins* or *santakas,* seeds and stems removed
3 tablespoons coriander seed
1 tablespoon black peppercorns
3 tablespoons poppy seed
2 teaspoons mustard seed
1 tablespoon cumin seed
1 tablespoon powdered turmeric
10 whole cloves
2 teaspoons cinnamon

Combine all ingredients in a spice mill and process to a fine powder.

Yield: About ¾ cup
Heat Scale: Hot

14

The North African Spice Bazaar

"The North African housewife can choose from up to 200 different spices and herbs when she stops to replenish her supplies at a spice stall in the *souks* [shops] of the *medinas* [native quarters]. There are no neatly labeled tins or boxes. These spices and flavorings from China, India, Java, Egypt, tropical Africa, Spain, and elsewhere in North Africa are offered whole and in bulk, displayed in large and small baskets and in 100-pound sacks. Naturally, many spices from this enormous array are used only rarely in special dishes. The North African cook relies mostly on cumin, caraway, garlic, coriander, saffron, wild ginger, white pepper, cinnamon, and the red peppers, which range in strength from hot to hotter to hottest. And there's mint, for mint tea."

Harva Hachten

ZAHTAR

This aromatic mixture from North Africa is also found in Turkey and Jordan. It is sprinkled over *tajines* and vegetables. Tunisian cooks make a paste of it with olive oil and spread it on bread before baking. The cayenne is optional. Sumac seeds are found in Middle Eastern markets.

2	tablespoons sesame seed	1	tablespoon powdered dried thyme
2	tablespoons dried sumac seed	1	teaspoon cayenne

Dry-roast the sesame seeds in a skillet over medium heat for a few minutes, stirring frequently. Allow to cool, then mix with the sumac, thyme, and cayenne.

Yield: ¼ cup

Heat Scale: Hot

TABIL

This spice mixture is from Tunisia, where it is sprinkled over grilled meats or used to spice up stews. The word *tabil* means "coriander," but generally refers to this blend of ingredients.

1	tablespoon coriander seed	2	cloves garlic
1½	teaspoons caraway seed	1	teaspoon dried crushed chile, such as *piquin*

Preheat the oven to 200 degrees. In a mortar, combine all ingredients and pound into a paste. Dry the paste on a plate in the oven for about 30 minutes. In a spice mill, grind the dried paste to a fine powder.

Yield: ⅛ *cup*

Heat Scale: Medium

WE'T SPICES

A *we't* or *wa't* is a traditional Ethiopian stew, spiced either with *Berbere* (see recipe, p. 25) or this simpler blend of spices. This spice mixture is usually added near the end of cooking a stew.

6 dried red New Mexican chiles, seeds and stems removed

3 tablespoons black peppercorns

3 tablespoons whole cloves

1 teaspoon ground nutmeg

½ teaspoon turmeric

In a dry skillet, toast the chiles, peppercorns, and cloves until they are aromatic, taking care not to burn them. Transfer to a spice mill and grind to a fine powder. Transfer to a bowl, add the nutmeg and turmeric, and mix well.

Yield: About ¾ cup

Heat Scale: Medium

VERY HOT ETHIOPIAN SPICES (MIT'MIT'A)

Mit'mit'a, another Ethiopian spice mixture, is also used to spice up and flavor stews, or *we'ts.* It is made from the small, hot African chiles that we know as *piquins,* and is sprinkled over raw meat (*kitfo*), especially lamb.

10	dried *piquin* chiles, seeds and stems removed	1	teaspoon ground cardamom
5	dried red New Mexican chiles, seeds and stems removed	1	tablespoon ground cloves
		1	teaspoon salt

Toast the chiles in a dry skillet, taking care not to burn them. Transfer to a spice mill and grind them to a powder. In a bowl, combine the dry chiles with the cardamom, cloves, and salt and mix well.

Yield: About ¾ cup

Heat Scale: Hot

CAPE MALAY SAMBAL

Many South African recipes are spiced up by *sambals* such as these that Malaysian immigrants brought to the country. Add it to grilled meats, soups, stews, and seafood dishes, or serve it over rice.

1½	cups vegetable oil	6	ounces peeled dried prawns (or shrimp)
4	medium onions, finely chopped	3	ounces tiny prawns (or shrimp), ground to a powder
6	tablespoons finely grated ginger root	1	tablespoon hot red chile powder
1	cup tomato paste		
2	cubes chicken bouillon		

Heat the oil in a saucepan and fry the onions and ginger for 10 to 15 minutes until the onions are golden. Stir in the tomato paste and mix thoroughly.

Crush the chicken bouillon cubes and add them to the pan, without water. Stir to mix. Simmer, stirring frequently, for 3 minutes. Add both types of prawns (shrimp) and stir for 1 minute. Add the chile powder and thoroughly blend in. Cook for 2 more minutes, stirring constantly. Take care not to burn the mixture at this stage.

Remove from the heat and let stand for about 1 hour or until the *sambal* has cooled down. Transfer to a storage jar and keep in a cool place until required.

Yield: 2½ cups

Heat Scale: Medium

MADAGASCAR SAUCE DYNAMITE

Judith Ritter, one of our correspondents, tasted Madagascar Sauce Dyna-mite when she visited L'Exotic, a Madagascar-style restaurant in Montreal, Quebec. She obtained the recipe for this typical sauce that spices up most of Madagascar's dishes. It keeps for up to a year in the refrigerator.

12	"bird" peppers (*chiltepíns* or *piquins*), crushed	¼	cup tomato paste
3	tablespoons freshly ground ginger	1	cup white vinegar
3	tablespoons freshly minced garlic	2	teaspoons salt
1	medium onion, diced	1	cup water
		1	tablespoon freshly chopped thyme

Mix all ingredients together in a pan. Bring to a boil, then reduce the heat and simmer for 15 minutes. Remove from the heat, cool, purée in a blender, and place the sauce in a small jar.

Yield: 2 cups

Heat Scale: Hot

HARISSA SAUCE

This classic sauce is thought to be of Tunisian origin, but it is found throughout North Africa. It is used to flavor couscous and grilled dishes such as kebabs. *Harissa* Sauce reflects the region's love of spicy combinations, all with a definite cumin and coriander flavor. Cover this sauce with a thin film of olive oil and it will keep up to a couple of months in the refrigerator.

10	dried whole red New Mexican chiles, stems and seeds removed		1	teaspoon ground cumin
	Hot water		1	teaspoon ground cinnamon
2	tablespoons olive oil		1	teaspoon ground coriander
5	cloves garlic		1	teaspoon ground caraway seed

Cover the chiles with hot water and let them sit for 30 minutes until they soften.

Place the chiles and remaining ingredients in a blender and purée until smooth, using the chile water to thin the mixture. The sauce should have the consistency of a thick paste.

Yield: 1½ cups

Heat Scale: Medium

A Mozambique Sauce-Making Class

"Of course every cook in Mozambique had his own particular way of preparing *piri-piri*. I have chosen one provided by a Portuguese housewife of Mozambique. According to her instructions, one begins by squeezing out some lemons, passing the juice through a sieve, warming it in a pan, inserting peppers and chiles that must be red (and freshly picked, she emphasized). They are simmered on a low heat for just five minutes. The mixture is then taken from the stove, separated from its juice, and the peppers pressed into a fine paste. A pinch of salt is added and the pounding continues until there are no lumps left in the pulp. The pulp is returned to the pan with the original lemon juice and further simmered while being constantly stirred. This, then, is the *piri-piri* sauce which can be eaten with steak, mutton, fowl, fish, and crustacean, and always best, I would say, with rice of some kind to provide the exact civilizing corrective to the pagan excitement of the sauce."

Laurens van der Post

BERBER BARBECUE SAUCE

This sauce for barbecuing poultry and meats originated in North Africa. It is named after the Berbers, a North African tribe who were renowned for their great skill as horsemen. This is great as a marinade and baste for grilled lamb chops.

1	tablespoon raisins	1	tablespoon ground peanuts
	Juice of one lemon		Pinch of chopped mint
5	tablespoons soft butter	1	teaspoon honey
⅔	cup peanut oil	¼	teaspoon dried basil
1½	teaspoons Malawi Curry Powder (see recipe, p. 14)	¼	teaspoon dried marjoram
½	teaspoon cayenne	¼	teaspoon dried allspice

Soak the raisins in the lemon juice for 15 minutes. Then add the butter, peanut oil, curry powder, cayenne, peanuts, mint, honey, basil, marjoram, and allspice to the bowl and mix well.

Yield: 1 cup

Heat Scale: Medium

BERBERE PASTE

Berbere is the famous—or should we say "infamous"—scorching Ethiopian hot sauce. One recipe we ran across called for over a cup of powdered cayenne! It is used as an ingredient in a number of dishes, as a coating when drying meats, and as a side dish or condiment. Tribal custom dictated that it be served with *kitfo,* raw meat dishes that are served warm. This sauce will keep for a couple of months under refrigeration. Serve sparingly as a condiment with grilled meats and poultry, or add to soups and stews.

4	whole cardamom pods	1	tablespoon ground cayenne
2	teaspoons cumin seed	2	tablespoons ground paprika
½	teaspoon black peppercorns	½	teaspoon ground ginger
½	teaspoon fenugreek seed	¼	teaspoon ground allspice
1	small onion, coarsely chopped	½	teaspoon ground nutmeg
4	cloves garlic	¼	teaspoon ground cloves
1	cup water	3	tablespoons vegetable oil
15	dried *piquin* chiles, stems removed		

Toast the cardamom, cumin, peppercorns, and fenugreek in a hot skillet, shaking constantly for a couple of minutes until they start to crackle and "pop." In a spice mill, grind these spices to form a powder.

Combine the onions, garlic, and ½ cup of water in a blender and purée until smooth. Add the chiles, cayenne, paprika, ground spices, and the ginger, allspice, nutmeg, and cloves and continue to blend. Slowly add the remaining water and the oil, and blend until smooth.

Remove to a saucepan and simmer the sauce for 15 minutes to blend the flavors and thicken.

Yield: 1 cup

Heat Scale: Extremely Hot

ETHIOPIAN GREEN CHILE PASTE (T'IQUR QARYA AWAZE)

This is the green chile counterpart to Ethiopian *Berbere,* but there are some differences: This one is green, it's much milder, and instead of placing it in stews, it's a condiment or dip for breads and meats.

2	bell peppers, seeds and stems removed, chopped	¼	cup vegetable oil
3	jalapeño chiles, seeds and stems removed, chopped	¼	teaspoon ground cardamom
½	tablespoon garlic	¼	cup chopped cilantro or Italian parsley
1	tablespoon minced ginger	½	teaspoon holy basil (optional)
			Water as needed

In a skillet, combine the bell peppers, jalapeños, garlic, ginger, and oil, and sauté until the bell peppers are tender—about 15 minutes. Drain the oil off and place the pepper mixture in a blender. Add the cardamom, cilantro, and holy basil and purée, adding enough water to make a thin paste.

Yield: About 1 cup

Heat Scale: Medium

26

Fire in the Jungle

"Our forebears must have had greater tolerance for hot seasonings than we. Contrast two travelers to West Africa a century
apart. Thomas Eyre Poole, the garrison chaplain for Sierra Leone
in the mid-19th century, was fond of upcountry excursions and
sometimes dropped unexpectedly into the hut of a friendly
villager at meal time. On his first sampling of a highly seasoned
meatball dish, he confided in his diary: 'These people know
what is good.' But in the 1950s an even more eager explorer,
Janheinz Jahn, dipped into his first meal in a Nigerian home and
almost screamed. 'I was on fire!' he wrote later. But he survived
and became an ardent propagandist for African cooking."

Ellen Gibson Wilson

WEST AFRICAN PILI-PILI SAUCE

Pili-pili, also called *piri-piri,* is served as a table condiment in all West African countries, where it heats up grilled meat, poultry, shrimp, fish, and even vegetable dishes. Nearly any green chile can be used to make this sauce. Some recipes call for tomatoes or tomato sauce to be added, and some recipes call for red chiles, either fresh or dried. This sauce will keep for two weeks, refrigerated.

1   pound serrano or jalapeño chiles, seeds and stems removed, coarsely chopped

1   medium onion, chopped
1   clove garlic
Juice of one lemon

Place all of the ingredients in a food processor and blend them into a paste, adding water until the desired consistency is achieved. Store in a jar in the refrigerator.

Variation: To make *Pili-Pili* Mayonnaise, combine 1 tablespoon of this sauce with 1 cup of mayonnaise and serve with cold, cooked, shelled shrimp or prawns.

Yield: 2 cups
Heat Scale: Hot

Pili-Pili in Kenya

"I took many meals in Mombasa at the excellent—though cramped and crowded—Big Bite restaurant on Maungano Road in New Town. Here I found cooks using spices like painters use colors. They spoke little English, but they were able to impart several recipes to me. My favorite was a hot sauce based on a spice blend and the juice of the Ukwaju, a native East African lemon. It's everywhere in Mombasa. The Portuguese are remembered for two things here: Fort Jesus and the *pili-pili* [pepper]. And when Fort Jesus is reduced by time and raindrops to a pile of dust, people will still be enjoying the *pili-pili.*"

Richard Sterling

PALAVER SAUCE

From Sierra Leone, here is one of the more unusual hot sauces we encountered. Besides palm oil, it is characterized by greens such as cassava or sweet potato leaves; spinach makes an adequate substitute. Some versions of this dish are more of a stew than a sauce, but this one is designed to be served over rice.

1 cup red palm oil (found in Asian markets), or substitute peanut oil

½ cup minced lean beef

1 onion, chopped

3 jalapeño chiles, seeds and stems removed, minced

2 cups shredded spinach

½ cup smoked fish, such as kippers

Heat the palm oil in a large skillet and fry the beef until just brown. Remove the beef and add the onion and jalapeños until soft, about 8 to 10 minutes. Add the spinach and stir-fry for 2 minutes. Return the beef to the skillet, crumble in the fish, and cook for 5 minutes over medium heat, stirring constantly. Add more palm oil if the mixture is too thick.

Yield: 2 cups

Heat Scale: Medium

SAUCE GOMBO

Gombo means okra in West Africa, and that vegetable is the primary thickening agent of this simple sauce from Ghana. The sauce can be served as a soup or poured over potatoes, plantains, or other starchy vegetables.

1 pound fresh okra, sliced into rounds	½ teaspoon salt
1½ cups water	1 tomato, coarsely chopped
2 teaspoons hot chile powder, such as cayenne	

Combine all ingredients in a sauce pan and cook over medium heat for 8 to 10 minutes, or until the okra is tender. Serve it as is or purée it in a blender for a smoother sauce.

Yield: About 2 cups

Heat Scale: Hot

NIGERIAN FRIED RED PEPPER SAUCE (ATA DINDIN)

Ata is the Yoruba word for chile pepper, and Nigerian chiles range from the tiny *ata wewe* to the large *ata funfun.* This sauce is served as a relish or dip with many West African dishes, particularly grilled meats. Thanks to D. Michael Warren for supplying this recipe, which he collected on one of his many trips to Nigeria.

10	dried red New Mexican chiles, seeds and stems removed	1	onion, chopped
½	cup peanut oil	1	can tomato sauce (8 ounces)
		1	teaspoon salt

Soak the chiles in hot water for 1 hour.

Remove the chiles from the water and purée them in a blender or food processor. Heat the oil in a skillet, add the onion, puréed chiles, tomato sauce, and salt. Fry over medium heat for 1 to 2 minutes, stirring constantly.

Variation: Add 1 chopped bell pepper and cook with the onion mixture.

Yield: 1½ cups

Heat Scale: Medium

32

A Subspontaneous Proverb

"In agricultural practice, chillies have, however, remained a subspontaneous crop [in Sudan], sown by birds. Azande have apparently never tried to extend their income from chillies by cultivating them. A Zande, once asked whether he preferred chillies to cotton as a cash crop, asked back, 'Do the birds sow my cotton?' implying the principle that your should never do for yourself what others can do for you."

Pierre de Schlippe, 1956

TSUMA NZOLE KALU'S SPECIAL SAUCE

This recipe was collected for us in Mombasa, Kenya, by Richard Sterling, who wrote: "The barbecue master at the Big Bite Restaurant in Mombasa is Tsuma Nzole Kalu. He concocted this recipe for hot sauce and gave it its name. Serve it over grilled or barbecued meats and poultry."

4	fresh *pili-pili* chiles or red jalapeños, seeds and stems removed
¼	teaspoon coriander seed
¼	teaspoon cardamom seed
1	teaspoon cumin seed
1	teaspoon black peppercorns

2	cloves
1	cinnamon stick
½	teaspoon salt
¼	cup water
1	Ukwaju Kenyan lemon or 1 lime, juiced

Combine the chiles, spices, salt, and water in a blender and purée to a thick paste. Transfer to a jar, and add the lemon or lime juice and enough water to make the mixture easily pourable. Shake well and set aside for a few hours to let the flavors blend.

Yield: About 1 cup

Heat Scale: Medium

UGANDAN GROUNDNUT SAUCE

Variations on this hot sauce appear all over Africa, with the key ingredient being peanuts in any form. Here, peanut butter works well—either smooth or crunchy. Its most common usage is to spread it over fried chicken or fish or to serve it over rice.

½ pound dried fish, such as
   salt cod, coarsely chopped
4½ cups water
2 teaspoons peanut oil
2 onions, chopped
4 tomatoes, chopped

2 teaspoons cayenne powder
1 teaspoon Malawi Curry
   Powder (see recipe, p. 14)
1 cup peanut butter
   Salt to taste

Soak the dried fish in 2 cups of water for approximately 1 hour, or until it becomes soft. Drain and pat dry.

   In a large skillet, fry the onions in the oil until brown, about five minutes. Add the tomatoes and cook uncovered for 5 minutes. Add the fish, cayenne, curry, remaining water, peanut butter, and salt. Simmer, uncovered, for 45 minutes, or until the sauce thickens to the desired consistency.

Yield: About 2 cups

Heat Scale: Medium

PUMPKIN HOT SAUCE (YEDUBBA WE'T)

There are many meat-based hot sauces in Africa, but also some distinctly vegetarian sauces such as this one from Ethiopia. Serve this sauce over starchy dishes such as plantains, yams, or rice.

1 cup vegetable oil	Salt to taste
1 cup chopped onion	4 cups cubed raw pumpkin
1 teaspoon crushed garlic	¼ teaspoon garlic powder
½ cup chopped red serrano chiles, or substitute jalapeños	¼ teaspoon ginger powder
¼ teaspoon cumin	5 cups water

In a skillet, brown the onions in the oil, stirring constantly to prevent sticking, for 5 to 10 minutes. Add the garlic, red chiles, cumin, and salt and cook for 20 more minutes, stirring occasionally. Add a little boiling water as needed to prevent sticking.

Add the pumpkin, garlic powder, ginger powder, and water, and bring to a boil. Cook until the pumpkin is tender. Purée in a blender for a smooth sauce.

Yield: 4 cups

Heat Scale: Medium

ETHIOPIAN CURRIED BUTTER (NIT'IR QUIBE)

This tasty clarified butter is a basic ingredient in the preparation of traditional Ethiopian foods. It also tastes great spread on toasted breads of any kind. In the refrigerator, it can be kept, covered, for three or four months.

1	3-inch piece fresh ginger, peeled and grated	1	tablespoon fenugreek seed
½	cup minced onion	2	teaspoons cumin seed
1	clove garlic, minced	1	tablespoon minced fresh basil
2	pounds butter	1	teaspoon cardamom seed
½	teaspoon cayenne	1	tablespoon fresh oregano
1	stick cinnamon	½	teaspoon turmeric powder
		¼	teaspoon ground nutmeg

Combine the ginger, onion, and garlic and pound to a coarse paste in a mortar. Set aside.

Melt the butter over low heat, stirring constantly, taking care that it does not darken. Skim off the foam as it rises, and continue cooking until all the foam is gone.

Add the paste and the remaining ingredients and simmer uncovered at the lowest possible heat, stirring occasionally, for 30 minutes.

Remove from the heat and allow to cool. Pour off the translucent top layer, leaving as much of the milk solids and spices as possible. Discard the solids. Strain the liquid through several layers of cheesecloth.

The clarified butter will usually be an oil at room temperature and solidify in the refrigerator.

Yield: About 2 cups

Heat Scale: Mild

YELLOW PEACH PICKLE

Pickles such as this one are commonly used in South Africa as a condiment to further spice up curries. Also serve as a relish with chicken, turkey, lamb, or fish. This will keep for one week in the refrigerator.

1	teaspoon peppercorns	1	teaspoon Malawi Curry Powder (see recipe, p. 14)
1	teaspoon coriander seed		
1	teaspoon whole allspice	1	teaspoon cornstarch
⅔	cup peach nectar (available canned in supermarkets)	½	cup chopped onion
		8	ripe peaches, peeled, pitted, and sliced
1	cup vinegar		
½	teaspoon salt	2	jalapeño chiles, seeds and stems removed, chopped
⅓	cup brown sugar		
½	teaspoon turmeric		

Tie the peppercorns, coriander seeds, and allspice together loosely in a muslin bag. Combine the peach nectar and vinegar, and soak the muslin bag in the liquid for 10 minutes.

Mix the salt, sugar, turmeric, curry powder, and cornstarch. Add ½ cup of pickle mixture (the spiced peach nectar and vinegar) and blend, then add to the pickle mixture, leaving the spice bag in. Cook in a saucepan until thickened, stirring constantly.

Add the onion, peaches, and chile pepper; cook for 10 minutes. Remove the spice bag, then pour the mixture into pint jars and seal.

Yield: 2 pints

Heat Scale: Medium

CAPE TOWN APPLE-RAISIN CHUTNEY

Here's a favorite Cape chutney that's served with curries and other South African dishes such as *bobotie* (curried casserole) and *sosaties* (kebabs).

3	pounds apples, peeled, cored, and chopped	1	fresh small green chile, such as serrano, seeds and stem removed, chopped
½	pound raisins, chopped	1	clove garlic, chopped
1½	quarts wine vinegar	2	tablespoons minced fresh ginger
1	cup sugar		
1	tablespoon salt		

Combine all ingredients in a large pot and simmer, uncovered, until thick—about 2 hours. Stir occasionally.

Spoon into sterilized jars and seal while hot. Serve at room temperature with curries.

Yield: 2 to 3 quarts

Heat Scale: Mild

A Chutney Primer

"Chutney is made by cooking fruit or vegetables with flavourings such as chillies, vinegar, garlic, ginger, and other spices until they form a pulp which may be thin enough to allow it to be poured, or quite thick. Traditional Cape chutney consists of apricots; it is thinner than other varieties and has a sweet-sour taste. Originally Malay chutney was extremely strong, but its potency was gradually reduced after it reached the Cape so that the spices were less overwhelming yet the characteristic fruit flavor was retained. These stimulating sauces continue to be popular in South Africa, especially when served with curry."

Renata Coetzee

Hot African Salads and Appetizers

Traditions and food often define the identity of nations. As the second largest continent after Asia, Africa conveys her long history and diverse peoples through her cuisine. Since the thirteenth century, Africans have shared their lands with nonindigenous folk, including Europeans, South Asians, Syrians, Lebanese, and many others. Each cultural group brought with them what they found most dear, which often included favorite spices, recipes, and preparation methods. Over time, these recipes and procedures have melded with the chiles, corn, fish, fowl, and other exotic foods available in Africa.

And so we begin our spicy journey with appetizers—first and second toasties, as they are called on this continent. The addition of appetizers to a meal is purely nontraditional; in fact, most traditional African meals are hearty enough to stand on their own, without additional savories. However, interesting starters are an important part of the contemporary cuisine of Africa, introduced by its immigrant population. Thus, this perennial party favorite is now often featured as a component of dinner and other festivities.

Our first three recipes—*Rougaille de Tomates* (p. 44), Madagascar *Pili-Pili* Dip (p. 45), and Green Mango Salad (p. 46)—are perfect examples of the blending of old with new. Reaching farther back in time, the recipe for White Cheese and Tomato "Salad" (p. 47) comes from ancient Egypt, collected by our good friend Richard Sterling on one of his many world adventures.

South Africa is the origin of our next sampling of appetizers. By land we offer South African *Samosas* (p. 48), borrowed from India to create hot and filling meat pies very similar to empanadas. By sea come three fabulous fish dishes: Garlic Cayenne Calamari with Nigerian Fried Red Pepper Sauce (p. 49), Cape Town Curry Capsicum Prawns (p. 50), and Steamed Crayfish with Cayenne-Spiced Butter (p. 52).

Next we venture to West Africa, with our first stop in Zaire. We begin with Avocado Smoked Fish with Hot Sauce (p. 51). Our next two selections, Feisty Fish Cakes (p. 54) and Smoky Hot Oyster Bites (p. 55), offer the perfect opportunity to vary the heat level of the cuisine by adding the hot sauce of your choice from Chapter 2.

Our next recipe is collected from Algeria: Two-Pepper Potato Cake (p. 56) packs a punch while showcasing the potato, one of the staple food items of Africa. The next recipe, *Berbere* Crackers (p. 57), is one of our favorites. It hails from Ethiopia, which is said to have the spiciest cuisine in all of Africa.

Who doesn't look for the dip upon arriving at a party? We've found three of the spiciest dips around for the sampling. We suggest the Pumpkin Dip (p. 58) from Tunisia and Curry Dip (p. 59) from Nigeria. Our final dip, Sesame Dipping Sauce (p. 60), offers an added bonus: It may actually bring you good luck, as Africans consider sesame seeds to be good-luck charms.

Powerful Plantains (p. 61) and Spicy Cape Meatballs (p. 62) are our next two recipes. These dishes also work well as main courses, so we suggest that you double the recipes and serve them together with a fruity dessert from Chapter 9 if you just can't seem to get enough of a good thing.

The English word "banana" came to America from Africa by way of the Portuguese explorers, with its spelling intact. Our next recipe, West African Banana and Chile Fritters (p. 63), features this fruit as well more than a hint of heat. Last, we return to West Africa to experience Fiery Yam Fritters (p. 64), Sweet-Hot Corn Cakes (p. 65), and Blistering Bean Balls (p. 66). Similar versions of these recipes are also found in the American South, which credits this area for much of its culinary roots.

ROUGAILLE DE TOMATES

This recipe is from our friend Judith Ritter, who often writes about the cooking of Madagascar. She sampled this salad at L'Exotic Restaurant in Montreal, Quebec.

2	fresh tomatoes, chopped	1	tablespoon chopped fresh parsley
2	shallots, minced		
½	onion, chopped	2	tablespoons olive oil
	Juice of ½ lemon		Salt and pepper to taste
1	tablespoon minced fresh ginger		Madagascar Sauce Dynamite (see recipe, p. 21) to taste

Combine all ingredients and serve over lettuce.

Yield: 4 servings

Heat Scale: Varies, depending on the amount of sauce you use

Early Egyptian Productivity

"By a thousand years after the first planting of crops in the Nile Valley, a new civilization had appeared and Egypt had entered on its first dynastic period. It is estimated that in the third millennium B.C. the Egyptian peasant was capable of producing three times as much food as he and his family needed to sustain them, which left a sizable surplus for feeding the armies of workers engaged on the flood-control projects, the public buildings, and the tombs designed to ensure a deferential welcome in paradise for Egypt's greatest nobles and dignitaries."

Reay Tannahill

MADAGASCAR PILI-PILI DIP

This hearty Madagascar recipe is a pâté of sorts—a very hot mixture spread over toast or crackers and served as an appetizer.

3   tablespoons vegetable oil

12 *pili-pili* chiles, or substitute other small, hot dried chiles, such as *piquins* or *santakas*

2   cups chicken livers

1   onion, minced

3   cloves garlic, minced

1   tablespoon fresh thyme

2   tablespoons green peppercorns

2   tablespoons minced fresh parsley

1   hard boiled egg, chopped
    Salt to taste

Heat the oil and sauté all ingredients until well cooked. Place in blender and blend until smooth.

Yield: 1½ cups

Heat Scale: Extremely Hot

GREEN MANGO SALAD

Here is our third Madagascar recipe from Judith Ritter. It is another unusual—and spicy—salad from L'Exotic Restaurant in Montreal.

3 jalapeño chiles, stems and seeds removed, minced

2 green mangos, pits removed, peeled and julienned

1 onion, minced

2 cloves garlic, minced

2 to 3 tablespoons minced fresh parsley

Juice of 2 limes

3 tablespoons olive oil

Salt to taste

Combine all ingredients and serve as a side dish with grilled or roasted meat or fish.

Yield: 4 to 6 servings

Heat Scale: Hot

New World Foods in Africa

"The most important contribution of Europeans to the African diet were crops imported from the New World. Maize, cassava, and peanuts became basic African foods. Crucial too were sweet potatoes, common and lima beans, Capsicums, pumpkin and squash, tomatoes, pineapples, papayas, guavas, avocados, and cashew nuts."

Raymond Sokolov

WHITE CHEESE AND TOMATO "SALAD"

When world traveler Richard Sterling collected this recipe in Egypt, he noted: "The Egyptians call any dish of raw vegetables a 'salad,' even though we would call this a dip or spread."

8	ounces feta cheese	1	pinch red New Mexican chile powder
2	teaspoons olive oil		
2	teaspoons lemon juice	2	tablespoons minced parsley
		1	large tomato, finely diced

Mash the cheese, oil, lemon juice, chile powder, and parsley together with a fork. Fold in the tomato.

Spread the mixture out on a serving plate and serve with pita toast points, crackers, or other crisp bread.

Yield: ½ cup

Heat Scale: Mild

SOUTH AFRICAN SAMOSAS

A "high tea" treat in South Africa, this spicy meat pastry of sorts originated in India but was transferred to South Africa by Indians who were brought to work on the South African railroads. Feel free to add more heat by increasing the amount of cayenne.

1	pound ground beef	1	teaspoon cayenne
3	green bell peppers, chopped	5	crushed cardamom pods
¼	teaspoon salt	1	teaspoon cinnamon
6	cloves garlic, finely chopped		Juice of 2 lemons
2	teaspoons caraway seed	1¾	pounds flour
1	pound onions, finely chopped		Oil for frying

Place the ground beef in a large bowl and add the chopped green peppers, salt, garlic, caraway, onions, cayenne, cardamom, cinnamon, and lemon juice. Combine thoroughly. Flour a surface suitable for rolling out dough. Place the meat mixture on the floured surface. Knead in one cup of flour at a time until all of the flour is kneaded in.

Next, form meat-dough balls about the size of a small meatball and fry on all sides in the oil until browned. Frying time is 10 to 15 minutes per batch. Drain on paper towels and serve warm.

Yield: 8 servings

Heat Scale: Mild

GARLIC CAYENNE CALAMARI WITH NIGERIAN FRIED RED PEPPER SAUCE

This South African recipe is a party favorite. However, take care to not over-cook the calamari; it turns from tender to tough and chewy very quickly, so remove it from the pan the moment it's done.

1½ pounds calamari tubes, thoroughly cleaned
½ cup flour
1 teaspoon ground black pepper
2 teaspoons cayenne
7 ounces butter
1 tablespoon oil
2 tablespoons crushed garlic
Lemon wedges for squeezing and for garnish
Nigerian Fried Red Pepper Sauce (see recipe, p. 32)

Slice the calamari into small pieces. Cut each piece in half lengthwise, lay flat, and score lightly in a diamond pattern. Next, season the flour with the black pepper and cayenne and toss the calamari in the flour mixture.

In a large, nonstick frying pan, heat the butter and oil until they start to brown. Stir in the garlic, add the calamari, and cook for 1½ to 2 minutes, depending on its thickness. Press the calamari down with a spatula to brown nicely. Cook the calamari in batches to control how quickly it cooks.

Transfer the calamari to a warmed serving platter and squeeze the lemon wedges over the top. Finally, spoon the sauce over the appetizer.

Garnish with lemon wedges and serve with rice.

Yield: 4 to 6 servings
Heat Scale: Medium

CAPE TOWN CURRY CAPSICUM PRAWNS

These butterflied, basted, grilled prawns are a sizzling sensation from South Africa. Serve with rice and the Green Mango Salad (p. 00), and make sure there are plenty of lime wedges for squeezing.

24 to 32 large prawns in shells
⅓ cup safflower oil
⅓ cup fresh lemon juice
2 teaspoons Dijon mustard
1 teaspoon Malawi Curry Powder (see recipe, p. 14)

2 jalapeños, stemmed, seeded, and chopped
Salt and ground black pepper
1 cup half-and-half
Lime wedges for squeezing

Slit the prawns down their backs, devein, and place with shell side down on a grilling tray. Heat the oven broiler.

Mix together the oil, lemon juice, mustard, curry powder, jalapeños, salt, and pepper. Brush this basting mixture over the prawns.

Grill for 4 to 5 minutes until cooked, then transfer the prawns to a warm serving platter. Peel before eating.

Pour the remaining basting mixture into the grilling tray, add the half-and-half, and cook on the stovetop until the sauce thickens to the correct consistency. Check the flavor and adjust if necessary. Pour the sauce over the prawns or offer it separately in small serving bowls. Squeeze limes over prawns before serving.

Yield: 4 servings

Heat Scale: Medium

AVOCADO SMOKED FISH WITH HOT SAUCE

This recipe is from Zaire, where it is known as "Senegalese Quiche." Feel free to choose another hot sauce from Chapter 2 to serve over this dish.

4	hard-boiled eggs	½	pound smoked fish, such as salmon, flaked
¼	cup milk		
¼	cup lime juice	2	large ripe avocados
¼	teaspoon sugar	1	red bell pepper, or 1 can pimentos, cut in strips
½	teaspoon salt		
⅓	cup vegetable oil	¼	cup West African *Pili-Pili* Sauce (see recipe, p. 28)
2	tablespoons olive oil		

Peel the hard-boiled eggs and take out the egg yolks. Mash the egg yolks in a large bowl. Mix in the milk and stir until it forms a smooth paste. Add 1 tablespoon of the lime juice, the sugar, and the salt. Mix well. Pour in the vegetable oil and the olive oil, then stir in the rest of the lime juice.

Make sure all skin and bones are removed from the flaked smoked fish. Chop the egg whites and mix them in a separate bowl with the fish. Then add the fish and egg whites to the sauce; toss gently and thoroughly, then refrigerate.

Just before serving, cut the avocados in half and take out the seeds and all the brown fibers. Spoon the refrigerated mixture into the avocado halves and top with either red pepper strips or pimento strips. Spoon the hot sauce over the dish and serve immediately.

Yield: 4 servings

Heat Scale: Medium

STEAMED CRAYFISH WITH CAYENNE-SPICED BUTTER

A wide variety of seafood is both extraordinarily popular and available in South Africa. This spicy starter features crayfish steamed in a mixture of wine, vinegar, and herbs, which is then reduced to form the base of a hot butter sauce. Please note: To preserve the succulent flavor, the crayfish must be freshly steamed and should not be refrigerated between steaming and serving. The sauce, too, should be freshly made and spooned over the crayfish while it is still warm.

8	crayfish tails (or substitute large shrimp)
4	ounces dry white wine
2	ounces white wine vinegar
1	fresh or dried bouquet garni (parsley, fennel, thyme)

Cayenne-Spiced Butter

Stock from poaching crayfish

4½ ounces cold butter, cut in small cubes

Freshly ground black pepper

1 teaspoon cayenne powder, or to taste

Cleaned leaves of butter lettuce

Sliced melon or papaya

Sprigs of parsley

Slice the crayfish tails by snipping down the length of the shell—both back and belly—with a pair of scissors. With a sharp knife, cut through the flesh and remove the vein canal. (Doing it this way is preferable to simply slicing through the shell, which tends to damage the flesh.)

In a medium saucepan, combine the wine, vinegar, and garni. Bring to a boil and add the crayfish, shells down. Cover and simmer very gently for 4 to 5 minutes, until the crayfish are perfectly cooked. Remove from the stock and cover with foil to keep warm while preparing the sauce.

To make the Cayenne-Spiced Butter, increase the heat under the stock and boil uncovered until it is reduced to about 2 tablespoons. Remove from the heat, discard the herbs, and whisk in the butter, a little at a time, until the sauce is silky smooth. Season with the ground pepper and cayenne.

Arrange the lettuce leaves on four serving plates. Remove the crayfish from the shells, place each piece on the lettuce, and spoon over just a touch of the Cayenne-Spiced Butter sauce. Garnish each serving with sliced melon and a sprig of parsley, and serve warm.

Yield: 4 servings

Heat Scale: Medium

And a Fiery Staff It Is

"All warm countries seem to favor hotly spiced food. Africans point out that [red] pepper preserves food, stimulates an appetite that might be dulled by the melting weather, and aids the digestion. The Yoruba proverb says: 'The man who eats no pepper is weak; pepper is the staff of life.' "

Ellen Gibson Wilson

FEISTY FISH CAKES

Fish is such a common, affordable food in West Africa that it's no wonder there are numerous recipes for spicy fish cakes. Try these served hot with any of the spicy dipping sauces from Chapter 2.

1½ cups potatoes, peeled and diced
Salt and fresh ground black pepper to taste
1 pound cooked fish fillets, skinned
¼ cup grated onion
1 tablespoon chopped parsley

½ teaspoon cayenne
A pinch of grated nutmeg
2 eggs, lightly beaten
Toasted crumbs for coating
Safflower oil for frying
Dipping sauce of choice from Chapter 2 (*piri-piri* sauce works well)

Cook the potato in a little salted water, drain, mash, and season with salt and pepper. Flake the fish and mix with the mashed potato, onion, parsley, cayenne, nutmeg, and beaten egg.

Drop spoonfuls of the fish cake mixture into the crumbs and coat evenly. Form the mixture into patties with your hands, flattening them slightly.

Fry the fish cakes in hot oil until they are crisp and golden. Remove from the oil and drain on paper towels.

Yield: 16 fish cakes

Heat Scale: Varies, depending on the dipping sauce you choose.

SMOKY HOT OYSTER BITES

These snacks from West Africa wrap canned oysters in crisp pastry for a quick and delicious taste sensation that may be served warm or cold.

1   package commercial puff pastry, such as Pepperidge Farm
2   cans smoked oysters, drained

Madagascar Sauce Dynamite (see recipe, p. 21)

Preheat the oven to 375 degrees. Lightly oil a baking tray. Roll out the pastry until thin and cut into circles about 3 inches in diameter. Place a smoked oyster onto each circle. Sprinkle some hot sauce over the oysters to taste. Fold the pastry over and seal the edges with a little water, crimping lightly with a fork.

Place the oyster bites on the baking tray and bake for 15 minutes or until golden-brown.

Yield: 20 oyster bites

Heat Scale: Hot

TWO-PEPPER POTATO CAKES

This recipe hails from Algeria, where it is a popular appetizer. Note the use of paprika here; it was introduced from Hungary via Spain. Feel free to spice it up further with any of the sauces from Chapter 2.

2	pounds mashed potatoes	1	bunch cilantro, chopped
1	tablespoon hot paprika pepper	3	eggs
2	teaspoons ground cumin		Salt and pepper
½	teaspoon cayenne		Oil for frying

In a large bowl, mix the potato with the spices, cilantro, eggs, and seasoning. With floured hands, form the mixture into round flat cakes. Cover and chill for 30 minutes.

Heat a shallow layer of oil in a frying pan, add the cakes in batches, and fry until crisp and brown on both sides. Transfer to paper towels to drain. Serve hot.

Yield: 4 to 6 servings

Heat Scale: Medium

BERBERE CRACKERS

These tangy tidbits from Ethiopia can be served as you would popcorn or peanuts, or they can be served with a dip from this chapter or a sauce from Chapter 2.

2	cups unbleached or whole-wheat flour	1	tablespoon sugar
2	tablespoons *Berbere* Paste (see recipe, p. 25)	1½	tablespoons salt
		⅔	cup water
		¼	cup safflower oil

Preheat oven to 350 degrees. In a bowl, combine the flour, *berbere*, sugar, and salt. Gradually mix in about ⅔ cup water until a thick paste forms.

Dump the mixture onto a floured board and knead it until you have a stiff dough. Make a well in the center of the dough ball and pour in the oil; fold dough over the oil and knead again until well mixed, about 5 minutes.

Covering the dough with a cloth to keep it moist, break off chunks to roll into ¼-inch-round strips. Cut the strips into ½-inch-long pieces, preferably using scissors so that the ends will be pinched.

Bake on a flat sheet or in baking tins for 20 to 30 minutes, until crisp. Stir three or four times to ensure even browning. When cool, store in airtight container.

Yield: 30 crackers

Heat Scale: Medium

PUMPKIN DIP (AJLOUKE ET POTIRON)

Tunisian *Harissa* and other spices transform the ordinary pumpkin into a characterful dish that is eaten cold with bread. Some African chefs even reserve the liquid from the pumpkin to use in soups or casseroles.

1½ pounds fresh pumpkin, or 24 ounces canned pumpkin

1½ tablespoons olive oil

¾ teaspoon caraway seed

¾ teaspoon ground coriander

½ teaspoon minced garlic

1 teaspoon *Harissa* (see recipe, p. 22), or more to taste

2 teaspoons lemon juice

Salt to taste

Peel the pumpkin and remove the seeds and threads. Chop the flesh and cook gently in a little water in a covered pan until tender. Drain thoroughly.

In a large pan, gently heat the oil. Add the caraway seeds and coriander, stirring occasionally until fragrant. Then add the pumpkin, garlic, *Harissa*, lemon juice, and salt. Remove the pan from the heat, mash all the ingredients together, then leave to cool.

Yield: 3 cups

Heat Scale: Medium

CURRY DIP

Indian immigrants, who worked building the railroads, popularized curries all over Africa. Serve this dip with raw vegetables or the *Berbere* Crackers (see recipe, p. 57).

1	cup mayonnaise	1	tablespoon grated onion
2	tablespoons prepared commercial salsa	1	clove garlic, minced
½	to 2 tablespoons Malawi Curry Powder (see recipe, p. 14)	¼	teaspoon salt
1	tablespoon Worcestershire sauce	¼	teaspoon black pepper

Blend all the ingredients until well combined. Chill.

Yield: 1 cup

Heat Scale: Mild

Exotic African Tourist Food

"Tourists like to return home and boast they ate a crocodile. It's better than the other way around," says Jan de Haast, a director of Zimbabwe's Sun Hotel chain. Other African "delicacies" being served to tourists include:

- Boiled elephant trunk
- Hippo burgers
- Flying ants fried in fat
- Field mice casserole
- Roast warthog

SESAME DIPPING SAUCE

This Middle Eastern dish is popular in Egypt and Sudan. It contains a lot of sesame seeds—one of the oldest plants grown for oil. In Africa, sesame is called *been* or *simsim*. Serve this dip with raw vegetables or crackers.

1 can chickpeas (16 ounces), drained	2 teaspoons lemon juice
	½ teaspoon salt
1 clove garlic, peeled	1 teaspoon cayenne
4 teaspoons sesame seed	½ teaspoon butter, softened

Put the chickpeas and garlic in a blender and purée until smooth. Scrape the mixture into a bowl and add the remaining ingredients, mixing well.

Yield: 3 cups

Heat Scale: Medium

POWERFUL PLANTAINS

Plantains, those banana relatives that are eaten as a vegetable, are cultivated in many African countries. This melange of sweet and hot plantains makes a delicious crunchy appetizer. Serve it with Ugandan Groundnut Sauce (see recipe, p. 35).

2	green plantains	2	yellow plantains
	Vegetable oil, for shallow	1	tablespoon garlic powder
	frying	¼	teaspoon salt
½	onion	2	teaspoons cayenne

Peel one of the green plantains and cut into very thin rounds, using a vegetable peeler.

Heat the oil in a large frying pan over moderate heat. Fry the plantain rounds in the oil for about 3 minutes, turning until golden brown. Drain on paper towels and keep warm.

Coarsely grate the other green plantain and put on a plate. Slice the onion into wafer-thin shreds and mix with the grated plantain.

Heat a little more oil in the frying pan and fry handfuls of the plantain-onion mixture for 2 to 3 minutes, turning once, until golden. Drain on paper towels and keep warm with the green plantain rounds.

Heat a little more oil in the frying pan. While it is heating, peel the yellow plantains, cut in half lengthwise, and dice. Sprinkle with garlic powder, salt, and cayenne pepper, and then fry in the hot oil until golden brown, turning to brown evenly.

Drain on paper towels and then arrange the three varieties of cooked plantains in shallow dishes. Sprinkle with salt and serve as a snack with your favorite hot sauce.

Yield: 4 servings

Heat Scale: Medium

SPICY CAPE MEATBALLS

From South Africa come these delicious kebabs, deliberately made small so that they fit the appetizer designation. Serve them with your favorite sauce from Chapter 2.

1	pound ground beef	2	teaspoons curry powder
1	egg	1	tablespoon lemon juice
3	garlic cloves, crushed	1	to 1½ cups fresh white bread crumbs
½	onion, finely chopped		
½	teaspoon freshly ground black pepper	1	small green chile, such as jalapeño, seeds and stems removed, minced
½	teaspoon ground cumin		Salt
½	teaspoon *dhania* (ground coriander)		Vegetable oil, for deep-frying
1	teaspoon ground ginger		

Place the ground beef in a large bowl and add the egg, garlic, onion, spices, lemon juice, about 1 cup of the bread crumbs, chile, and salt.

Using your hands or a wooden spoon, mix the ingredients together until the mixture is firm. If it feels sticky, add more of the bread crumb and mix again until firm.

Heat the oil in a large heavy pan or deep-fat fryer. Shape the mixture into balls or fingers and fry, a few at a time, for 5 minutes or until well browned all over.

Using a slotted spoon, drain the kebabs and then transfer to a plate lined with paper towels. Cook the remaining kebabs in the same way and then serve, if you like, with a spicy dip from this chapter or a sauce from Chapter 2.

Yield: 6 servings

Heat Scale: Medium

WEST AFRICAN BANANA AND CHILE FRITTERS (KAKLO)

This is one of the more unusual vegetarian African appetizers. Note the combination of bananas, chiles, and ginger that makes for a sweet and spicy flavor.

2	bananas	½	teaspoon salt
1	small onion, chopped	1	teaspoon grated ginger
1	tomato, chopped	1	cup flour
½	green chile pepper, such as jalapeño, stem and seeds removed, minced	2	tablespoons water Peanut oil for frying

Peel the bananas and mash. Add the onion, tomato, and chile pepper and mash again. Add the salt and ginger. Mix the flour and water, then add to the banana mixture and stir well.

Heat the oil until hot enough for deep-frying. Drop the mixture half-teaspoonfuls at a time into the oil and fry until golden brown. The balls should be crisp on the outside, but soft on the inside. Serve as hot or cold snacks, or hot with a main dish.

Yield: 4 servings

Heat Scale: Medium

FIERY YAM FRITTERS

Here is another popular fritter from West Africa with two sources of chile heat. Serve them with a dip from this chapter or a sauce from Chapter 2.

1½	pounds yams	½	teaspoon salt
1	medium-size onion, chopped fine	¼	teaspoon pepper
1	medium-size tomato, chopped fine	¼	teaspoon thyme A pinch of cayenne pepper
1	green chile, such as jalapeño, seeds and stems removed, minced	1 ½	egg, beaten cup bread crumbs Peanut oil for frying

Boil yams with skins on until tender; peel and mash smooth. Sauté onion, tomato, and green chile in a few tablespoons of oil until brown. Add seasonings and sautéed mixture to yams. Add egg and bread crumbs and mix well.

Form into small patties and sauté in peanut oil until brown on both sides.

Yield: 4 to 6 servings

Heat Scale: Medium

SWEET-HOT CORN CAKES (AKPETE)

These interesting corn cakes from Ghana can be eaten hot or cold, alone or with roasted peanuts, for a snack or appetizer.

2	cups white cornmeal	3	tablespoons sugar
⅔	cup all-purpose flour	2	tablespoons peanut or other vegetable oil
½	teaspoon cayenne		Water as needed
2	teaspoons baking powder		Peanut oil for deep-frying
1	teaspoon salt		

Combine the dry ingredients and oil in a bowl, then add just enough water to form a stiff dough. Shape into egg-sized oval cakes and dust lightly with flour.

Heat the oil to 350–375 degrees. Fry the cakes, a few at a time, until well browned. Drain on paper towels.

Yield: 1½ dozen cakes

Heat Scale: Mild

Pepper Problems in Zimbabwe

"The main problem with pepper growing, said Deck Mafukidze, was its nasty habit of itching on hands during harvesting. Termites and goats also found the crop quite palatable. However, these were not serious problems and extension officers were always on hand to provide services on nursery production, transplanting, pesticide use, harvesting, and distributing."
The *Harare Herald,* 1995

BLISTERING BEAN BALLS

These bean balls from West Africa can be consumed hot or cold, as a snack or as a side dish. Some West Africans eat them with Nigerian Fried Red Pepper Sauce (see recipe, p. 32) for breakfast. Others sprinkle the balls while hot with additional red pepper, or press crushed dried chile pods into them.

2 cups white beans or black-eyed peas	½ teaspoon ground ginger (optional; used in Ghana)
1 medium onion	1 teaspoon salt
1 *fatalii* chile (or substitute habanero), seeds and stem removed, minced	Peanut or other vegetable oil for frying (traditionally palm oil)
1 egg, beaten	

Soak the beans or peas overnight.

Drain the beans or peas and pound them with a pestle or masher to loosen the skins, floating them off in running water. Alternatively, spread them on a board and use a rolling pin to rub the skins loose. Soak further, if necessary, until the beans or peas can be crushed. Grind, purée in an electric blender (adding water as needed), or pound to a smooth consistency.

Grind or grate the onion and chile very fine, and add to the beans or peas. Add the egg and seasonings, and beat the mixture thoroughly to incorporate some air.

Heat the oil to 350–375 degrees. Drop the mixture by spoonfuls into the hot oil and fry until deep brown. Drain on paper towels.

Yield: 3 dozen

Heat Scale: Hot

Biriani *and* Chop:
Soups and Stews

Soups and one-dish meals seem to proliferate all over the world—everything goes into one pot. Not only are these dishes simple and easy, but you can stretch the food supply as far as possible by adding lots of vegetables and starches. In this chapter, we have included soup and stew variations from all over Africa, from the simple, almost vegetarian dishes to those that are more complex in ingredients as well as cooking procedures.

The first group of recipes are the simplest, but nonetheless very tasty. Nigerian Yam Soup (p. 71) contains both potatoes and yams, and is enriched by the addition of some cream. The African yams, which look like large, coarse potatoes, have been replaced in this recipe by a combination of potatoes and American yams. The American "yams" add to the color and taste of the finished dish.

Curried Coconut Soup (p. 72) is another easy, interesting West African dish. In it, the richness of the coconut is offset by chicken stock and freshly ground ginger. A similar dish is made by many cooks in the Caribbean. This is no surprise, considering that many of the slaves brought to the New World were from the West African coast.

From North Africa, we offer Tunisian Chickpea Soup (*Lablabi,* p. 74), which would traditionally be served as a main supper dish. Don't let the large amount of garlic worry you; the longer garlic cooks, the mellower the flavor gets. Many varieties of peanut soup (or groundnut soup) are popular all over Africa, especially in the west, due to the high protein content of peanuts. Our version of Peanut-*Piquin* Soup (p. 73) is slightly spicier than most, thanks to the addition of dried *piquins,* and richer than most, thanks to the addition of some cream.

Since avocados are abundant in Africa, we have included a recipe for Chilled Avocado Soup (p. 76), which is made spicy by fresh green chiles and piquant by the addition of fresh lime juice. The lime juice also helps to acidify the soup and keep it from turning brown. Red Chile Papaya Soup (p. 77) is a typical South African recipe because so much fresh produce is grown in this fertile, productive area. Fruit juice soups and chunky fruit soups are very popular, spiced with a dash of hot sauce or some ground chile.

The next section of soups and stews are those containing chicken. Chicken Groundnut Stew (*Hkatenkwan,* p. 78) once again contains peanuts, this time in the form of peanut butter. The addition of chicken pieces, hot Thai peppers for a spicy touch, and okra are typical of a West African recipe. Since okra is called "gombo" in Swahili, the next recipe, Chicken and Okra

Stew or African Gumbo (p. 79), is appropriately named. Okra was brought to the New World by the African slaves. This soup is simple in ingredients, but high in flavor with tomatoes, cayenne pepper, and okra.

The influence of India is present in the recipe for Curried Chicken and Banana Soup (*Supu Ya N Dizi,* p. 80); a healthy dollop of curry is added, along with some tasty coconut and dried red pepper. Ethiopian Chicken Stew (p. 82) is a highly spiced stew, typical of Ethiopia and East Africa. This stew is traditionally eaten with *Injera* Bread (see recipe, p. 217), also called "the daily bread, tablecloth, and silverware" because it serves all of those purposes. This dish is fun to serve at parties, especially after a few glasses of wine, because you get to watch your friends try to eat with just the bread and their fingers.

The *Biriani* (p. 84) is Indian in origin, transferred to South Africa by the numerous East Indians who were brought to work in the area. This recipe is rich in spices, and requires long, slow cooking to meld the seasonings with the meat. Curry Beef Soup (p. 83) is another recipe from South Africa that carries an Indian influence. It is a great one-pot meal.

Some say that Steak Stew with Rice (p. 86) is made in the same manner as paella, with its vegetables and rice, although this dish packs quite a punch with the use of crushed red chiles. Nigerians love their food hot and spicy, and this recipe is no exception. Another red chile delight is Beef Groundnut Chop (p. 88). *Chop* is an African slang term for "food" or "meal." Peanut butter provides the rich, hearty sauce for this spicy one-pot meal. The heat of this dish is tempered nicely by the many condiments that can accompany it; the fruit and the vegetables add to the flavor, while allowing the diner to consume something hotter than ever imagined.

No one knows why Sierra Leone Pepper Soup (p. 90) is so named, since it doesn't contain any more chile peppers than many of the other soups. Some versions of this recipe in Nigeria call for fish instead of meat, and use potatoes instead of rice. The recipe allows many variations on a theme, depending on what you have on hand. Another soup that can have many versions is Out of Africa Lentil Soup (p. 87). The soup is rich with spices and chile and makes a very satisfying one-pot meal. Lentils are sometimes called "portable protein" because dried lentils travel well.

We have included two lamb recipes from North Africa, and the first is the aromatic Lamb *Tajine* with Fruit and Honey (p. 92). This exotic recipe contains fruit, honey, spices, and a touch of cayenne. In North African food traditions, it is the Persians who are credited with combining fruit and meat. The distilled orange-flower water adds another unusual taste treat. Orange-flower water is imported from France or Lebanon, and is available in gourmet shops.

Another North African or Maghreb dish is Lamb and Vegetable Soup with Vermicelli (*Chorbah,* p. 94), which contains a multitude of ingredients, including apricots, tomatoes, red chile, and mint leaves. The fruit and mint harken back to the Middle Eastern influences on North African cuisine.

The last group of recipes encompasses both fish and seafood. Shrimp and Okra Stew (*Ila,* p. 96) contains simple ingredients, but when they are combined they make this dish something special. This Nigerian recipe is typical of the unusual combinations of ingredients found in many African recipes—what's fresh, what's available, and what would taste good together.

The Crab and Green Chile Stew (*Kotokyim,* p. 97) from Ghana is another simple yet very hot and flavorful seafood dish containing tomatoes, chiles, and crab. It is excellent served over cooked rice. Simplicity and robust taste are also found in Fish and Eggplant Stew (*Froi,* p. 98). This stew contains not only fish fillets but also shrimp, eggplant, and a hearty dash of red chile flakes.

One North African recipe, Chunky Tunisian Fish Soup (p. 100), is a substantial meal in itself. It is made of fish and shellfish, and spiced with *harissa.* Serve this rich soup with good, crusty bread to sop up all of its juices.

Haddock and Orange Broth (p. 102), from South Africa, borrows the cooking styles of the Cape Malay and Asia: Fish combined with fruit juice, spices, red chile, and a garnish of fresh cilantro. The rich fishing waters of the South provide an abundance of both fish and seafood, and these figure prominently in the cooking traditions of the people who live near the coast.

The last recipe, Swahili-Style Seafood Soup (p. 101), contains all of the ingredients of a truly exotic meal: fish, seafood, coconut milk, curry, and chiles. For extra food raves, add several dashes of home made *piri-piri* chile sherry (see recipe, p. 221) just before serving. Enjoy trying some of these exciting recipes!

NIGERIAN YAM SOUP

This delicious, thick, yellow soup is rich in flavor and chiles. Serve it as a first course and serve the fruity Lamb *Tajine* (p. 92) as the entrée.

2 tablespoons peanut oil	1½ pounds yams or sweet potatoes, peeled and cut into 1-inch cubes
1 cup chopped onion	
½ cup chopped carrot	3½ cups beef stock
4 fresh jalapeño or serrano chiles, seeds and stems removed, and minced	½ teaspoon salt
	¼ teaspoon freshly ground black pepper
1½ cups chopped tomatoes	½ cup half-and-half cream
½ pound potatoes, peeled and cut into 1-inch cubes	Chopped parsley for garnish
	Freshly grated ginger for garnish

Heat the oil in a large, heavy casserole; add the chopped onion and carrot and sauté for 1 minute. Then add the chiles, tomatoes, cubed potatoes, and cubed yams and sauté and toss for 1 minute.

Add the beef stock, salt, and pepper, and bring the mixture to a boil. Reduce the heat to a simmer, cover, and simmer for 30 minutes.

Remove the soup from the heat, allow it to cool for 20 minutes, and then purée it in a food processor or blender. Do this in batches if necessary.

Return the soup to the casserole and bring to a boil. Reduce the heat to a simmer and add the cream in a steady stream, stirring constantly.

Serve the soup hot and garnish with the parsley and ginger.

Yield: 4 to 5 servings

Heat Scale: Medium

CURRIED COCONUT SOUP

The use of curry is a more recent addition to West African recipes. Curry mixes well with the many classical African ingredients to create modern versions of traditional foods. The hot curry powder creates a tangy Nigerian soup, which is tempered by the mild taste of coconut milk.

3	cups coconut milk	1	tablespoon freshly grated ginger
3	cups chicken stock	1	teaspoon cornstarch
2	teaspoons Malawi Curry Powder (see recipe, p. 14)	½	cup plain yogurt
½	teaspoon salt		Minced parsley for garnish
¼	teaspoon freshly ground white pepper		
¼	cup packaged grated coconut, plus ¼ cup toasted coconut for garnish		

Combine the coconut milk and 2¾ cups of the chicken stock in a large, heavy casserole and bring to a boil. Reduce the heat slightly and add the curry powder, salt, pepper, grated coconut, and ginger, and simmer for 10 minutes.

Mix the cornstarch with the reserved stock and add it in a steady stream to the simmering soup, stirring constantly until the soup thickens slightly.

Serve the soup hot with a dollop of yogurt, and sprinkled with the toasted coconut and parsley.

Yield: 4 to 6 servings

Heat Scale: Medium

PEANUT-PIQUIN SOUP

Each African country seems to have its own version of peanut soup, or groundnut soup. It is common all over Africa, but it is especially popular in the western part of the continent. The soup can be made a day ahead to blend the flavors, and then carefully reheated.

1	pound shelled, roasted peanuts	8	cups beef or chicken stock
1	tablespoon peanut oil	¾	cup milk
1	cup chopped onion	1	tablespoon cornstarch
½	cup chopped carrots	¾	cup cream
3	dried, crushed *piquin* chiles, or 3 fresh jalapeños with seeds and stems removed, minced	½	teaspoon salt
			Chopped parsley for garnish
			Chopped chives for garnish

Rub the skins off the peanuts. Place the nuts in a food processor and grind them to a very fine meal. Set aside.

Heat the oil in a large casserole and sauté the onion and carrots for 2 minutes. Add the chiles, the ground peanuts, and the stock and bring the mixture to a boil. Lower the heat and simmer uncovered for 1 hour, stirring occasionally.

Pour ½ cup of the milk into a small jar, add the cornstarch, and shake vigorously. Pour the mixture through a fine sieve into the soup and then stir continuously for 1 minute. Then add the remaining milk, the cream, and the salt. Simmer for 3 minutes, not allowing the mixture to boil. Cover the soup and let it simmer for 30 minutes.

Serve the soup hot, garnished with the parsley and chives.

Yield: 6 servings

Heat Scale: Mild

TUNISIAN CHICKPEA SOUP (LABLABI)

This thick and delicious soup from North Africa should be served as a supper dish, which is when many thick, spicy soups are traditionally served. Even though ten cloves of garlic sounds like a lot, the garlic mellows as it cooks. Serve it with crusty warm bread.

1 pound dried chickpeas	1½ tablespoons red chile powder or chile caribe
¼ cup olive oil	½ teaspoon ground cumin
1 cup chopped red onion	1 teaspoon hot paprika
10 cloves garlic, slightly crushed	10 cups chicken stock or water
¾ cup chopped carrots	2 tablespoons fresh lemon juice
1 cup chopped celery	3 tablespoons chopped cilantro
1 teaspoon salt	
¼ teaspoon freshly ground black pepper	

Pick over the chickpeas (removing any small pieces of stone or other debris), cover them with water, and soak them overnight in the refrigerator.

Drain the chickpeas and place them in a very large casserole or stock pot. Cover with fresh, cold water and bring the mixture to a boil. Reduce the heat to a simmer, cover, and cook for 30 to 40 minutes or until the chickpeas are just tender.

While the chickpeas are cooking, heat the oil in a large skillet and add the onion, garlic, carrots, celery, salt, black pepper, red chile powder, cumin, and paprika. Sauté the mixture slowly for 3 minutes, then cover and simmer for 10 minutes. Remove from the heat.

Drain the chickpeas, pour them back into the large casserole, and add the sautéed vegetable mixture. Add the stock and stir until all is well mixed.

Spoon about ½ of the mixture into a food processor or blender and purée. Return the purée to the soup and reheat. When the soup is hot, stir in the lemon juice and the cilantro. Serve immediately.

Yield: 6 to 8 servings

Heat Scale: Medium to Hot

The Other Kind of Bush Food

"There is something rather incongruous about the five-course meals served by lodges in the middle of the bush. White-coated waiters pass the food with impeccable style, permitting each diner to select from a choice of soups, fish, meat, vegetables, and desserts. Dinner is usually rounded off by a sampling of Kenyan cheeses, and sated guests finally retire to the glassed-in viewing areas to sip Kenyan coffee and liqueurs while watching the animals in the wild, miles from civilization."

Kathy Eldon and Eamon Mullan

CHILLED AVOCADO SOUP

This Pan-African soup is both cold and hot at the same time. The chiles add the heat, yet it is very refreshing in hot weather because chiles help to cool down the body. Serve it as a first course with fresh bread.

4	ripe avocados, peeled and mashed	¼	teaspoon freshly ground white pepper
5	cups chicken stock, with fat removed	3	serrano or jalapeño chiles, seeds and stems removed, minced
1	tablespoon fresh lime juice		
½	teaspoon salt	1½	tablespoons minced scallions or chives

Mash the avocados in a large bowl, add the stock, lime juice, salt, pepper, and chiles, and mash until the mixture is semi-smooth. If you like a velvet texture, place the mixture in a blender or food processor and purée. Chill the soup for several hours.

Garnish the soup with the scallions or chives.

Yield: 4 to 5 servings

Heat Scale: Medium

RED CHILE PAPAYA SOUP

Even though the papaya is a native of the Western Hemisphere, papayas have been cultivated all over the world in semitropical zones. The exotic flavor of this fruit combines with dried red chile and mace to give it a most wonderful taste in this South African recipe.

2	tablespoons butter	½	teaspoon salt
1	cup chopped onion	¼	teaspoon freshly ground white pepper
½	cup chopped parsley		
2	teaspoons red chile powder	⅛	teaspoon ground mace
1½	pound papaya, peeled, seeded, and coarsely cubed	3¼	cups milk
		2	teaspoons cornstarch
1	cup papaya juice		Toasted croutons for garnish

Heat the butter in a large skillet and sauté the onion for about 3 minutes, until it is a golden color. Add the parsley, chile powder, cubed papaya, papaya juice, salt, and pepper, and simmer over low heat until the mixture resembles a pulp.

Position a sieve over a large saucepan, pour the papaya pulp into the sieve, and press down on the contents to get all of the liquid into the saucepan. Add the mace.

Add 3 cups of the milk and heat the mixture gently, not allowing it to boil.

When the mixture is hot, mix the cornstarch and the remaining ¼ cup of milk in a small jar and shake. Pour the cornstarch through a fine sieve into the hot soup and stir until the soup is slightly thickened. Simmer for 3 minutes over a low heat.

Serve hot with croutons.

Yield: 4 servings

Heat Scale: Mild

CHICKEN GROUNDNUT STEW (HKATENKWAN)

Groundnut or peanut soups and stews are extremely popular in the cooking of Ghana and Mali in West Africa. In fact, some consider them to be the most popular of all Sunday meals. Chicken is usually the preferred meat, but we have found that a variety of meats and seafood are also used, including beef, lamb, smoked fish, and crab.

1	cup water	2	tablespoons tomato paste
10	to 12 pieces of chicken, rinsed and drained	1	cup tomato pulp
¼	cup grated fresh ginger	1	teaspoon salt
2	teaspoons hot curry powder	½	teaspoon freshly ground black pepper
2	tablespoons crushed dried Thai chiles, or other hot dried red pepper	6	cups chicken stock or water
1	cup chopped onion	1	pound eggplant, peeled and cut into 1-inch cubes
¾	cup peanut butter	1	cup fresh or frozen okra
			Diced pimentos for garnish

Pour the water into a large sauté pan. Add the chicken, ginger, curry powder, chiles, and onions, and sauté the mixture for 15 minutes, turning several times.

While the chicken is cooking, mix together the peanut butter, tomato paste, tomato pulp, salt, and pepper, and stir them into the chicken mixture. Add the chicken stock, bring the mixture to a boil, reduce the heat, cover, and simmer for 30 minutes.

When the chicken is tender, add the eggplant and the okra and simmer for 10 minutes, stirring twice. If the stew is thickened enough, serve it immediately with the pimentos as garnish. If the stew still has too much liquid, simmer it uncovered for several minutes.

Yield: 6 to 8 servings

Heat Scale: Hot

CHICKEN AND OKRA STEW, OR AFRICAN GUMBO

Okra is frequently used in African stews as a thickening agent, and it was African slaves who brought okra to the New World.

4	pounds chicken, cut apart into legs, thighs, and breasts	4	cups chopped tomato
	Flour for dredging	4	cups chicken stock
3	tablespoons peanut oil	1	pound okra, cut into 1-inch thick rounds
2	cups chopped onion	1	tablespoon flour (if needed)
1	teaspoon salt	¼	cup warm water (if needed)
2	teaspoons cayenne		

Wash the chicken and pat the pieces until they are dry. Place the flour in a paper or plastic bag and dredge the chicken, a few pieces at a time.

Heat the oil in a large, heavy casserole. Add the chicken pieces, a few at a time, and brown them.

Add the onion, salt, cayenne, tomato, and stock and bring the mixture to a boil. Reduce the heat to a simmer, cover, and cook until the chicken is tender, about 50 to 60 minutes.

When the chicken is tender, add the okra and simmer for 10 minutes. The okra should thicken the stew. If the stew is not thick enough, mix the flour with the water and stir into the stew.

Yield: 4 to 6 servings

Heat Scale: Medium

CURRIED CHICKEN AND BANANA SOUP (SUPA YA N DIZI)

This recipe is from Tanzania, East Africa. While soups and stews are common throughout Africa, this recipe shows an Indian influence by the addition of curry powder and coconut.

4	pounds chicken, cut apart into legs, thighs, and breasts	1	teaspoon freshly ground black pepper
3	tablespoons peanut oil	1	tablespoon ground or crushed red chile
3	cloves garlic, minced		
1	cup chopped onion	2	cups chopped tomato
2	cups chopped celery	1	cup shredded coconut
2½	tablespoons hot Madras curry powder (available in gourmet or specialty stores)	1½	quarts chicken stock
		2	slightly underripe bananas, sliced
1½	teaspoons salt		

In a large, heavy casserole, brown the chicken in the oil. Drain the chicken on paper towels and set aside.

Sauté the garlic, onion, and celery in the oil for 1 minute. Add the curry powder, salt, black pepper, and red chile, and sauté for 1 minute.

Add the chicken to the sautéed vegetables and add the tomato, coconut, and chicken stock. Bring the mixture to a boil, reduce the heat to a simmer, cover and cook for 40 minutes until the chicken is very tender.

Remove the chicken pieces and take the meat off the bones. Return the meat to the simmering stock mixture, then add the banana and simmer for 10 minutes.

Yield: 6 servings

Heat Scale: Medium

Tanzania, We Presume

"This is the finest place I have known in all of Africa to rest before starting my final Journey. An illusive place where nothing is as it seems. I am mesmerized. . . ."

David Livingstone, 1866

ETHIOPIAN CHICKEN STEW

Ethiopian food is unique in its flavors, being spiced with chiles rather than curry. When you have a chance to eat at an Ethiopian restaurant, go with several people and order different dishes—and make sure to include Ethiopian Chicken Stew. You will find that the meal includes *Injera* Bread (see recipe, p. 217), which is used to scoop up the food, rather than using forks. Be sure to serve the stew with *Injera* Bread when you make it.

6 pounds chicken pieces, skin removed	¼ cup *Berbere* Paste (see recipe, p. 25)
½ cup butter	1 teaspoon salt
½ cup vegetable oil	¾ teaspoon freshly ground black pepper
4 cloves garlic, minced	8 hard-boiled eggs, shells removed
3 cups minced onion	
1 can (6 ounces) tomato paste	

Pierce each piece of chicken with a fork several times.

Heat the butter and vegetable oil in a large, heavy casserole; add the garlic and onion and sauté for 2 minutes. Then add the tomato paste, *berbere*, salt, and pepper and simmer, stirring occasionally, for 5 minutes.

Add the chicken pieces and toss to coat with the sauce. Add just enough water to barely cover the chicken, bring the mixture to a boil, cover, reduce the heat and simmer for 30 minutes.

Add the hard-boiled eggs and simmer for 20 minutes, keeping the liquid at the consistency of a thick soup. If the mixture gets too thick, add water.

Cut the eggs in half, return them to the stew, and serve immediately.

Yield: 8 to 10 servings

Heat Scale: Medium

CURRY BEEF SOUP

This soup recipe originated in South Africa, and the curry flavor is thought to have come from the many East Indians brought into South Africa to work on the railroads.

2	tablespoons vegetable oil	1	teaspoon salt
1½	cups chopped onion	¼	teaspoon freshly ground black pepper
1	pound beef, cut into ½-inch cubes	2	cups cubed potatoes, ¾ inch thick
7	cups beef stock	2	tablespoons cider vinegar
3	tablespoons Malawi Curry Powder (see recipe, p. 14)		Chopped cilantro or chopped scallions for garnish
2	whole bay (laurel) leaves		

Heat the oil in a large, heavy casserole. Add the onion and the beef and sauté until the beef is browned, about 2 minutes. Add the stock, curry powder, bay leaves, salt, and pepper. Bring the mixture to a boil, then reduce the heat to a simmer, cover, and cook for 30 minutes.

Stir in the potatoes and vinegar, cover, and simmer for 45 minutes to 1 hour, until the beef is tender.

Serve hot with the cilantro or scallions as garnish.

Yield: 6 servings

Heat Scale: Medium

BIRIANI

Slow cooking is the key to a good *biriani.* The Indian origins of this South African dish are evident in the many spices that are included. This is frequently served at weddings and other celebrations.

2	pounds lamb or beef	½	teaspoon cinnamon
2	tablespoons vegetable oil	½	to 1 cup water, plus 4 cups water
2	cloves garlic, minced	2	tomatoes, peeled and sliced
3	cups chopped onion	2	cups rice
2	teaspoons salt	1	strand saffron (½ inch), crushed
1	teaspoon cayenne	1	tablespoon butter
1	tablespoon grated fresh ginger		
½	teaspoon dried, crushed fennel		
3	cardamom seeds, crushed		

Cut the meat into bite-sized pieces and set aside.

Heat the oil in a skillet and sauté the garlic and onion until the onion starts to wilt, about 2 minutes.

Place the meat in a large, heavy casserole and add the sautéed mixture, 1 teaspoon of the salt, the cayenne, ginger, fennel, cardamom, and cinnamon, and ½ cup of water. Layer the tomatoes on top. Cover and simmer over a very low heat for 30 minutes, or until the meat is nearly cooked.

Bring 4 cups of water to a boil and add the rice, saffron, and the remaining teaspoon of salt. Cover, reduce the heat to a simmer, and cook for 20 minutes. When the rice is done, stir in the butter.

Preheat the oven to 250 degrees.

Grease the bottom of a large, heavy casserole with a little oil. In the casserole, layer ⅓ of the rice, ½ of the meat mixture, ⅓ of the rice, the remaining meat mixture, and finally the remaining rice. Sprinkle the top with water. Cover tightly and place the casserole in the oven.

Bake slowly for 1½ hours, checking to see that there is always a little moisture in the casserole; sprinkle with more water if necessary.

Yield: 6 to 8 servings

Heat Scale: Medium

Bacteria Beware

"When I first arrived to work in Malindi, I was told by my sister's African Muslim driver (he's part African, part Arab/Swahili) that folk wisdom states that if I eat a chile pepper with each meal, I will never get food poisoning. As a former bus driver, he's eaten in lots of unhygienic places, and swears by this method. At first, I supposed that was because if your stomach can handle chiles, it can also handle a few bacteria. Later, in *Chile Pepper* magazine, I learned about the antibiotic effects of chile on bacteria, so African folk wisdom is proved by science."

Michelle Cox

STEAK STEW WITH RICE

Variations on this famous Nigerian dish appear all over West Africa, including versions made with game, fish, chicken, and vegetables.

4½	cups water	1¼	cups chopped onion
1	teaspoon salt	2½	cups chopped tomatoes
2	pounds sirloin steak, cut into 12 pieces	3	tablespoons tomato paste
5	tablespoons peanut oil, or vegetable oil	3	teaspoons crushed red chiles or red chile caribe
		1	cup rice

Heat ½ cup of the water and ½ teaspoon of the salt in a large, heavy skillet. Add the steak pieces and simmer, turning the meat once or twice, until the water is evaporated. Add 3 tablespoons of the oil and brown the meat. Set the meat aside.

Place the remaining 2 tablespoons of oil, 2 cups of the water, 1 cup of the onion, 2 cups of the tomatoes, 2 tablespoons of the tomato paste, and the chile in a large, heavy saucepan and bring to a boil. Add the reserved meat, reduce the heat to a simmer, and cook until the mixture thickens, stirring occasionally.

Heat the remaining 2 cups of water and the remaining ½ teaspoon of salt in a saucepan. When the water is boiling, add the rice and the remaining onion, tomatoes, and tomato paste. Cover and simmer for 20 minutes.

To serve, spoon the rice over the meat.

Yield: 6 servings

Heat Scale: Mild

OUT OF AFRICA LENTIL SOUP

Lentils have always been a source of protein in parts of Europe, much of the Middle East, and India. They were probably brought to Africa by the spice traders, and they have been utilized in cooking since the time of the ancient Egyptians and the Sumerians. They are a simple staple that can take on a lot of seasoning and spice.

½	pound green lentils	7	cups chicken stock
2	tablespoons olive oil	1	cup chopped carrots
1	cup chopped onion	½	cup chopped celery
3	cloves garlic, minced	1	cup diced potatoes
½	pound veal or beef shin, chopped	1	teaspoon salt
½	teaspoon cinnamon	¼	teaspoon freshly ground white pepper
¼	teaspoon cumin	2	tablespoons fresh lemon juice
2	teaspoons cayenne	½	cup chopped cilantro

Place the lentils in a large, heavy casserole and cover them with cold water. Bring the water to a boil, reduce the heat to a light rolling boil, and cook for 10 minutes. Drain the lentils and set aside.

Heat the oil in a large skillet; add the onion and sauté for 1 minute. Add the garlic and the veal and sauté for 30 seconds, stirring frequently. Stir in the cinnamon, cumin, and cayenne. Pour this mixture into the large casserole with the lentils and add the chicken stock. Bring the mixture to a boil, skimming the residue off the surface. Cover and simmer for 1 hour until the meat is tender.

Add the carrots, celery, potatoes, salt, and pepper, and simmer for 30 minutes.

Just before serving, stir in the lemon juice and the cilantro.

Yield: 6 to 8 servings

Heat Scale: Medium

BEEF GROUNDNUT CHOP

This recipe makes a big meal. It contains some of the most basic ingredients of West African dishes, with garnishes similar to those served with East Indian curry dishes. In West Africa, the beef would probably be replaced by wild game, buffalo, or antelope. Use your imagination here in North America and substitute elk, venison, antelope, or lamb. Serve the huge pot of stew and the wonderful condiments buffet-style.

2 tablespoons vegetable oil	3 tablespoons chile caribe (crushed dried red chile)
5 pounds beef or game, cut into 1-inch cubes	2 cups hot water
4 cups coarsely chopped onion	½ pound peanut butter
1 teaspoon salt	28- or 32-ounce can stewed tomatoes
½ teaspoon freshly ground black pepper	6 hard-boiled eggs, chopped

Heat the oil in a large, heavy Dutch oven or stockpot and add the meat in batches to brown. When almost all of the meat is browned, add 2 cups of the onion and sauté until wilted, about 2 minutes.

Stir in the salt, black pepper, and chile. Add the hot water and bring the mixture to a boil. Reduce the heat to medium, and, stirring a few times, allowing the water to reduce by half.

Add the remaining onions and just enough hot water to cover the meat plus ½ inch, and simmer for 25 minutes, covered.

Scoop out about 2 cups of the broth and place it in a small bowl. Add the peanut butter and whisk the mixture until it is smooth. Gradually add this mixture to the simmering meat, stirring to keep the sauce smooth. Add more hot water if the mixture looks too thick.

Add the tomatoes and the chopped eggs, bring the mixture to a boil, reduce the heat to a simmer, cover, and cook for 45 minutes or until the meat is tender. Stir the mixture occasionally and add more hot water if it starts getting too thick.

Serve the dish with hot, cooked rice, and any or all of these condiments: fried plantain pieces, chopped tomatoes, chopped bell pepper, chopped oranges, toasted coconut, fried onion rings, chopped roasted peanuts, mango chutney, crushed red pepper, diced papaya, grated ginger root, fried okra, and chopped boiled eggplant.

Yield: 10 servings

Heat Scale: Hot

Hot Love

"A husband can tell how much his wife loves him by how much hot pepper is in his food. If it is bland to his taste, she doesn't love him any more and he is very hurt. She must use the hot spice with a heavy hand to assure him of her devotion."

Bea Sandler

SIERRA LEONE PEPPER SOUP

This is a simple but delicious soup. People tell us that this soup is given to people with head colds—the "African Penicillin Beef Soup Remedy," just as chicken soup is the American remedy! The chiles in this soup will certainly clear the sinuses, whether you have a cold or not.

1	tablespoon vegetable oil	1	teaspoon dried thyme
1	pound stewing beef, cubed	¼	cup tomato paste
4	serrano or jalapeño chiles, stems and seeds removed	1	teaspoon salt
1	large onion, peeled and quartered	¼	teaspoon freshly ground black pepper
½	pound tomatoes, peeled and sliced		Hot cooked rice

Heat the oil in a large, heavy casserole; add the beef and brown it for 2 minutes, tossing the whole time. Add enough water to cover and bring to a boil for 2 minutes. Skim off any residue, reduce the heat to a simmer, cover, and cook for 30 minutes.

Place the chiles and onion in a food processor or blender and purée. Add this mixture to the meat as it is cooking.

Stir the tomatoes, thyme, tomato paste, salt, and pepper into the simmering beef mixture. Cover and simmer for 1 hour, adding more liquid if necessary.

Serve the hot soup over cooked rice immediately.

A Nigerian recipe for Ibo Pepper Soup calls for fish instead of meat. In this dish, peppers and onion are ground together first and cooked five minutes in boiling water before the fish and some fresh, sliced okra are added. The mixture cooks a further 20 minutes.

Another Pepper Soup recipe from Sierra Leone uses ¾ pound of fresh fish or a large fish head and adds three white potatoes, thickly sliced.

Yield: 4 servings

Heat Scale: Medium Hot

And We Thought Dinner For Four Seemed Like a Lot

"In the Cape Malays, a good cook or *motjie-kok* is highly regarded in the community and is often asked to cook for weddings and funerals, where she presides in unquestioning glory. She usually has a team of women who will clean, fetch, and carry while she cooks, often for more than 1,000 guests."

Cass Abrahams

LAMB TAJINE WITH FRUIT AND HONEY

Of all the African cuisines, North African is probably the best known in the United States. This Moroccan recipe reflects the influence of history. When the Moors returned to Morocco after occupying Spain, they brought with them a love of fruit and meat dishes. The sweetness of the fruit is countered by the addition of spices and black pepper.

2 pounds lamb or chicken, cut into 2-inch cubes	1 clove garlic, minced
1 teaspoon ground cayenne	½ teaspoon freshly ground black pepper
½ teaspoon ground ginger	1 pound plums, apples, pears, or prunes
1 strand saffron (½ inch), crumbled	¼ cup honey, preferably orange blossom
½ teaspoon ground cumin	1 teaspoon distilled orange-flower water
2 tablespoons olive oil	¼ cup toasted sesame seeds
1 tablespoon fresh lemon juice	
1 cinnamon stick (2 inches)	
1 cup chopped onion	

Combine the meat, cayenne, ginger, saffron, cumin, olive oil, lemon juice, cinnamon, onion, garlic, and black pepper in a large, heavy casserole. Add just enough water to barely cover the meat, bring the mixture to a boil, reduce the heat to a simmer, cover, and cook for 30 minutes.

Remove the cover and simmer an additional 30 minutes, until the meat is tender. If the meat is not tender and the liquid is disappearing, add a small amount of water and continue to simmer. Remove the cinnamon stick.

While the meat is cooking, prepare the fruit. If you are using plums or prunes, pit them but leave them whole. If you are using apples or pears, core and quarter them, but do not peel them.

When the meat is tender, stir the fruit into the meat mixture and simmer over a very low heat for 12 minutes.

Add the honey and the orange-flower water and bring the mixture to a boil for a few seconds. Turn off the heat, serve, and sprinkle each serving with the toasted sesame seeds.

Serve over hot, saffron-infused rice (crush a ¾-inch saffron thread into the cooking water when preparing the rice).

Yield: 4 to 6 servings

Heat Scale: Mild

Madagascar Heat

"Chef Jean-Louis Themis [of L'Exotic Restaurant, Montreal] was born and raised on the African island of Madagascar. He is exuberant when he talks about the role of chiles in his country's cuisine. 'It's medicinal. It's an aphrodisiac. It's delicious. The pepper is king!' Madagascar grows many varieties of peppers, but the most famous is the little 'bird pepper.' In Malagasy (the country's language), the pepper's name is *'tsy lany dimy laihy.'* That means 'even five men can't finish it.' "

Judith Ritter

LAMB AND VEGETABLE SOUP WITH VERMICELLI (CHORBAH)

Two thousand years ago, the Maghreb consisted of Morocco, Tunisia, Algeria, and Libya. Even today, despite being divided into separate countries, the countries in the former Maghreb area share variations of this soup recipe. Some sources even claim that dwellers of this area created dried pasta as a method of preserving starchy food for long treks through the desert. This recipe makes a delicious and unusual soup, easy to prepare, and certain to excite the taste buds of your guests.

3	tablespoons olive oil	2	tablespoons crushed, dried red chile
2	pounds lamb, cut into 1-inch cubes	2	cups chopped tomatoes
2	cups chopped onion	½	cup dried apricots, cut into quarters
2	cloves garlic, minced	2	tablespoons chopped mint
2	red bell peppers, chopped	¾	cup broken, dry vermicelli
2	lamb bones, cracked	2	tablespoons fresh lemon juice
8	cups chicken stock		Chopped parsley for garnish
1	teaspoon salt		Chopped mint for garnish
¼	teaspoon freshly ground black pepper		

Heat the oil in a large, heavy casserole and add the lamb. Brown the lamb, then push it to one side of the casserole. Add the onion, garlic, and bell pepper and sauté for 1 minute.

Add the cracked bones, stock, salt, black pepper, chile, tomatoes, apricots, and mint. Bring the mixture to a boil, then reduce the heat to a simmer, cover, and cook for 1½ hours, until the lamb is tender.

Then bring the mixture to a boil, add the vermicelli, and boil gently for 6 minutes until the vermicelli is cooked. Turn off the heat and add the lemon juice. Serve with the parsley and mint as garnishes.

Yield: 6 to 8 servings

Heat Scale: Medium

SHRIMP AND OKRA STEW (ILA)

The interesting combination of shrimp and bananas gives this West African dish an exotic flair. It is light and delicious.

3 tablespoons peanut or vegetable oil	½ pound cooked shrimp or prawns
1 cup chopped onion	Juice of 1 fresh lime or lemon
1 pound fresh or frozen okra, sliced into ½-inch rounds	1 teaspoon cayenne
1 large ripe banana, cubed	1 teaspoon salt
5 medium tomatoes, peeled and chopped	¾ cup water

Heat the oil in a casserole, add the chopped onion, and sauté for 1 minute.

Cut the tops off of the okra and slice thinly. Frozen okra should be thawed just enough to slice. Add the okra to the sautéed onions.

Add the cubed banana and the tomatoes to the onion mixture and simmer for 3 minutes.

Mash the shrimp in a bowl with a potato masher and add the lime juice, cayenne pepper, and salt. Then add this mixture to the onion mixture. Add ¾ cup of water, cover, and simmer for about 25 minutes, checking the water level to be sure it doesn't dry out.

Serve with hot, cooked rice.

Yield: 4 servings

Heat Scale: Mild

CRAB AND GREEN CHILE STEW (KOTOKYIM)

This dish from Ghana is delicious and easy to make. The hot chiles are balanced by the tomatoes and the crab.

1	onion, peeled and cut into quarters	1	pound cooked crab meat, flaked
3	to 4 hot green chiles, such as serrano or jalapeño, seeds and stems removed	½	teaspoon salt
		½	teaspoon freshly ground white pepper
2	tablespoons peanut oil	¾	cup tomato juice or V-8 juice
2	cups chopped tomatoes		Minced parsley for garnish

Place the onion, chiles, and oil in a food processor or blender and mince finely. Heat a deep skillet, add the minced mixture, and sauté for 1 minute.

Add the tomatoes and sauté until soft. Then add the crab meat, salt, white pepper, and tomato juice and simmer for 15 minutes, covered.

Garnish with minced parsley and serve with hot, cooked rice.

Yield: 4 servings

Heat Scale: Hot

FISH AND EGGPLANT STEW (FROI)

The blending of eggplant (often called "garden eggs") and fish creates a unique taste treat from Ghana, with an additional surprise from the shrimp. Because the eggplant is salted to remove excess moisture, go easy on any additional salt when cooking this dish.

2	pounds sole or flounder fillets	1½	cups peeled, coarsely cubed tomatoes
2	teaspoons commercial poultry seasoning	2	teaspoons chile caribe or red chile flakes
1½	pounds eggplant, peeled, and cut into 1-inch cubes	¼	teaspoon freshly ground white pepper
	Salt	½	pound shrimp (any size), shelled and deveined
3	to 4 tablespoons olive oil	1	cup water
1	medium green bell pepper, chopped		
1	cup chopped onion		

Wash the fish under cold running water and then pat them dry with paper towels. Sprinkle the fillets with the poultry seasoning and set aside.

Place the cubed eggplant in a sieve and sprinkle liberally with salt. Place the sieve in the sink and allow the eggplant to sit for 30 minutes. Then rinse off the salt under cold running water. Place the eggplant between several layers of paper towels or a linen kitchen towel and gently squeeze out any excess moisture.

Heat the oil in a large, heavy skillet, add the eggplant, and sauté for 1 minute. Add the bell pepper and onion and sauté for 1 minute longer. Add the tomatoes and continue sautéing until the onions are very wilted.

Preheat the oven to 350 degrees.

Stir the dried chile and the pepper into the eggplant mixture. Reduce the heat to a simmer, cover, and cook for 4 minutes. Remove the skillet from the heat, allow it to cool slightly, then put the sautéed mixture in a food processor and purée.

Pour the puréed mixture into a large, heavy casserole. Layer the fish fillets over the mixture and place the shrimp on top of the fillets. Gently add 1 cup of water, cover, and bake for 25 to 35 minutes.

Yield: 4 servings

Heat Scale: Medium

CHUNKY TUNISIAN FISH SOUP

Tunisia has one of the richest fishing areas in North Africa. Any kind of fish and shellfish can be used in this recipe, but avoid oily fish such as mackerel and sardines. There are many parallels between this fish soup and bouillabaisse, which is popular in southern France.

2 tablespoons olive oil	2 cups diced potatoes
2 cups chopped onion	3 tablespoons fresh lemon juice
1 red bell pepper, chopped	6 cups fish stock
1 red chile, such as serrano or jalapeño, seeds and stem removed, minced	4½ pounds mixed fish and shell-fish, washed and cleaned
3 cloves garlic, minced	4 cups chopped tomatoes, seeded
2 teaspoons *Harissa* (see recipe, p. 22)	½ cup chopped cilantro
½ teaspoon cumin powder	½ cup chopped parsley
⅛ teaspoon saffron threads	1 teaspoon salt
1 fennel bulb, diced	½ teaspoon freshly ground white pepper

Heat the oil in a large, heavy casserole. Add the onion, bell pepper, chile, and garlic, and sauté for 2 minutes, stirring occasionally.

Stir in the *harissa,* cumin, saffron, fennel, potatoes, lemon juice, and fish stock. Bring the mixture to a boil, reduce the heat to a simmer, cover, and cook for 15 to 20 minutes, until the potatoes are tender.

Add the fish, tomatoes, cilantro, parsley, salt, and pepper, and simmer for 20 to 30 minutes, until the fish is tender.

Yield: 6 to 8 servings

Heat Scale: Medium

SWAHILI-STYLE SEAFOOD SOUP

This recipe was given to us by Michelle Cox of the Driftwood Beach Club in Malindi, Kenya. You can go to the resort to have this soup, or you can make it at home. She suggests a dash of *piri-piri* sherry (see recipe, p. 221) to the finish off the soup. And if you don't care for coconut, she suggests that you add 2 more cups of fish stock. Thanks, Michelle; this recipe is

1½ pounds uncooked fish and seafood (any mixture, depending on your budget)	2 Kenya chiles, or jalapeños, seeds and stems removed, chopped
4 tablespoons oil or butter	1 teaspoon salt
1 cup chopped onion	¼ teaspoon freshly ground black pepper
½ pound carrots, finely chopped	
½ pound leeks, finely chopped	4 ripe plum tomatoes, peeled and chopped
½ pound celery, finely chopped	
1 teaspoon chopped garlic	2½ cups coconut milk (available in cans)
¼ cup dry white wine	
1 teaspoon curry powder	3 to 4 cups fish stock
Pinch of saffron	¼ cup chopped cilantro
	Juice of 2 limes

Clean and cube the fish and the seafood. Set aside.

Heat the oil in a large, heavy pot; add the onions and sauté for 1 minute. Add the carrots, leeks, celery, and garlic and sauté for 2 minutes.

Add the fish and seafood, wine, curry powder, saffron, chiles, salt, and pepper, and bring to a simmer. Add the tomatoes, coconut milk, and fish stock; return to a simmer and cook slowly for at least 10 minutes, or until all of the vegetables are tender. Then stir in the cilantro and lime juice.

Yield: 4 to 6 servings

Heat Scale: Mild

HADDOCK AND ORANGE BROTH

South African cooking has incorporated many cooking styles, including Cape Malay and Asian, thus accounting for the spices and chiles in some recipes. The rich fishing waters provide a variety of fish and seafood. Serve this soup with warm *Roti* bread (p. 218). *Roti* is the Malay word for "bread."

3	pounds haddock fillets	½	teaspoon freshly ground white pepper
2	tablespoons butter	¼	cup dry sherry
1	fresh red chile, such as serrano or jalapeño, seeds and stem removed, minced	½	cup cream
1½	cups sliced carrots	½	teaspoon salt
1	cup chopped onion		Milk as needed
½	cup fresh orange juice		Minced coriander leaves for garnish
1	teaspoon grated orange zest		Julienned strips of orange rind for garnish

Place the fish in a large skillet, cover with water, and poach for 25 to 35 minutes, until the fish flakes easily. Remove the fish from the water, flake the fish, and set aside, reserving the poaching liquid.

Heat the butter in a saucepan and add the chile, carrots, and onion and sauté for 3 minutes. Stir in the reserved poaching liquid, orange juice, zest, and pepper. Cover and simmer for 15 to 25 minutes, or until the carrots are soft.

Remove the pan from the heat, uncover, and allow it to cool for a few minutes.

Pour the contents of the saucepan into a food processor or blender and purée the mixture. Return the puréed mixture to the saucepan and add the reserved fish, sherry, cream, and salt. Heat the mixture slowly to avoid boiling the cream. If the mixture seems too thick, add a tablespoon or more of milk.

Serve in warm bowls, topped with the coriander and orange rind.

Yield: 6 to 8 servings

Heat Scale: Mild

Bobotie, Kefta, and Other Meat Dishes

The major players in this chapter are beef and lamb, with a veal and a chicken-beef-ham recipe thrown in for good measure. Pork is seldom mentioned in African cooking, perhaps due to the continental population of Muslims who, according to the Koran, are prohibited from eating pork.

The lamb tradition goes back to an old adage: When in doubt, serve lamb; it is acceptable to almost everyone, regardless of their religious association. And, in many ways, the same is true for goat, if it is available in your area.

The multitude of beef recipes reflects the low number of Hindus in Africa. Beef is second to lamb or goat as the preferred meat to serve.

Very few chicken recipes are included in this chapter. Chicken is more frequently stewed in a large one-pot meal (see Chapter 4), rather than being served as the centerpiece of the meal, because, with the addition of vegetables and starches, it can go farther to feed more people. (Also see Chapter 6 for poultry.)

The first recipe is from North Africa. Lamb Couscous with Onion and Raisins (p. 108) is rich in spices and honey; with *harissa* on the side, diners can spice their own dishes. Spiced Lamb with Apricots (p. 110) is typical of the melding of fruit and meat also found in North African cooking. In this Tunisian recipe, the lamb is combined with fruit juice, fruit, cilantro, and mint, with *harissa* served at the table to add at will.

Lamb and Cayenne *Kefta* (p. 112), another North African lamb recipe, hails from Morocco and includes a variety of spices, cayenne, and a Moroccan favorite: fresh mint. The mint brings all of the flavors and the heat together, and when it is grilled and served in pita bread, the taste is wonderful.

Tajines can be either stews or casseroles, and the next recipe, Lamb *Tajine* Roast with Cayenne and Herbs (p. 114), is the latter. The lamb is highly seasoned with garlic, spices, and cayenne, and the best part of this dish is that you can eat it traditionally—with your fingers. It's a great party centerpiece. The next *tajine*, Lamb *Tajine* with Chestnuts and Chickpeas (p. 113), is Tunisian. It, too, is highly seasoned with spices and chile. The addition of the chestnuts and chickpeas add an unusual touch to this dish.

South Africa has its lamb specialties, too, and the first one is *Sosaties* (p. 116), which is a spiced, skewered, grilled dish, similar to a Malay *saté* (spiced, grilled meat with hot sauce). It is delicious, and easy to make and serve. Boer Lamb Chops Marinated in a Spicy *Sambal* (p. 118) is a popular South African dish spiced with Cape Malay *Sambal* and dry mustard. Serve this dish with a full-bodied South African red wine. Another South African dish, *Bobotie* (p. 120), also deserves a good red wine. It is like a spicy lamb mini-soufflé, spiced with Malawi Curry Powder, garlic, and ginger, and tempered with chutney and fruits.

Pinang-Kerrie (p. 122) is the all-time favorite South African curry, made with Malawi Curry Powder, turmeric, ginger, tamarind, and chiles. It has its origins in the Cape Malay cooking traditions. Lamb and *Mchicha,* a One-Dish Meal (p. 123) is a unique recipe contributed by Richard Sterling. It is easy to prepare and wonderful to serve with its spices and chiles; the coconut milk gives a dash of richness. Leg of Lamb in Hot Sauce (p. 124), from Ethiopia, is spiced with *berbere* and seasoned with cardamom, garlic, and ginger. Serve it cooked, or serve it raw—your choice. We have included one main-course beef-and-chicken recipe in this chapter—*Jollof* Rice (p. 125). This recipe is rich with cayenne, smoked ham, and a myriad of vegetables.

Another simple and delicious recipe from West Africa, Marinated and Grilled Round Steak (*Tsitsinga,* p. 126) consists of grilled beef cubes rolled in roasted corn flour. Beef *Berbere* (p. 127), from Ethiopia, is cooked in red wine and spiced up with *berbere* sauce; the use of cardamom gives this dish an exotic taste. A variation of this recipe calls for turmeric, which adds a lovely golden color. Ethiopian Ground Beef with Peppers (p. 128) is another tasty beef recipe from East Africa.

Pepper-Peanut Beef Kebabs (p. 129), from Nigeria, is another simple yet very delicious beef dish. It contains only four ingredients—red chile, beer, beef, and peanuts—and it will delight everyone's palate. A similar recipe, West African Beef Kebabs (p. 130), contains not only sirloin, but cubed liver as well as chiles and ginger. Both of these dishes are as popular in West Africa as hot dogs are in the United States.

Papaya Ginger Beef with *Piri-Piris* (p. 132) is a delicious stir-fry dish from East Africa. It makes the most of locally available ingredients, including chiles, papaya, and ginger. The papaya acts as a tenderizer, as well as an aid for digestion, so this dish is indeed good for you.

Romazava (p. 131) is considered the national dish of Madagascar. The beef is sautéed with ginger, and fresh, leafy vegetables are added just before serving. The heat in this dish comes from Madagascar Sauce Dynamite (p. 21).

This chapter is rounded out with one veal recipe—Spicy Veal Casserole with Tomato Topping (p. 134)—which is a Somalian casserole containing fresh chiles, herbs, and fresh tomatoes.

LAMB COUSCOUS WITH ONIONS AND RAISINS

We thank Rosemary Ann Ogilvie for giving us this recipe. She says, "This recipe by the manager of the Salaam Hotel in Morocco, like most of the recipes I gathered, feeds a number of people. You can, however, reduce it by cutting the ingredients in half. Serve with a side of *harissa* chile paste [see recipe, p. 22] to increase the heat."

2	pounds boneless lamb, cubed
2	medium onions, sliced
2	tablespoons olive oil
2	quarts water
1	bunch cilantro, tied together with a string
¼	teaspoon crushed saffron threads
1	teaspoon ground turmeric
4	cups cubed pumpkin or squash, unpeeled
3	tablespoons butter or margarine, plus 1 tablespoon butter

2	teaspoons ground cinnamon
2	teaspoons ground ginger
2	tablespoons slivered almonds
2	tablespoons sugar, or 3 tablespoons honey
1½	cups raisins, soaked in warm water and drained
2	teaspoons ground red New Mexican chile
3	cups beef broth
1	pound uncooked couscous Salt and pepper to taste

Brown the lamb and half of the onions in the oil. Place in a large pot along with the water and the cilantro, saffron, ½ teaspoon of the turmeric, and the pumpkin cubes. Bring to a boil, reduce the heat, cover, and cook until the pumpkin is tender, about 1¼ hours.

Remove the pumpkin; when it is cool enough, peel the skin off and set the pumpkin flesh aside. Remove the cilantro, cover the pot, and continue cooking until the lamb is tender. Set aside.

Sauté the remaining onions in 3 tablespoons of the butter, and add the cinnamon, ginger, almonds, sugar, raisins, the remaining turmeric, and the chile powder. Cover and cook over a very low heat for 30 minutes. Set aside.

Bring the broth to a boil. Place the couscous in a large bowl and pour the broth over the grain. Cover and allow to stand until all the liquid is absorbed. Mix in the remaining tablespoon of butter and use a fork to separate the grains and fluff them up. Cover and keep warm until serving time.

Pile the couscous on a large plate. Make a hole in the center of the mound, place the pumpkin and lamb inside the well, top with the onion-and-raisin mixture, and serve with salt and pepper.

Yield: 6 to 8 servings

Heat Scale: Mild

Antelope Dinners

- The largest African antelope is the eland, which can weigh more than 1,200 pounds. It has been semidomesticated and is used as a draft animal and a source for milk and meat; it makes for excellent eating.
- "Thomson's gazelle, whose meat, prepared in the African manner by being marinated in berries and wine before being roasted with a basting of banana gin, is said to be of intoxicating excellence."

Waverly Root

SPICED LAMB WITH APRICOTS

We recommend that you buy your apricots at a natural foods store. Shopping in a North African spice souk or bazaar, you can find as many as 200 different spices and herbs from all over the world, including chile peppers, which can be some of the hottest around.

⅓	cup orange juice, freshly squeezed	⅛	teaspoon freshly grated nutmeg
4	tablespoons olive oil	1½	pounds lamb, cubed
3	cloves garlic, minced	8	dried apricots, soaked in water overnight in refrigerator
2	tablespoons minced fresh cilantro	1	cup chopped onion
2	tablespoons *Harissa* (see recipe, p. 22), plus additional *harissa* to serve on the side	¼	cup chopped dried dates
		2	cups chicken stock
2	tablespoons minced fresh mint	3	tablespoons toasted sesame seeds
½	teaspoon ground cumin		

Mix the orange juice, 2 tablespoons of the oil, garlic, cilantro, *harissa*, mint, cumin, nutmeg, and lamb together in a shallow glass (Pyrex) casserole dish. Cover and marinate overnight in the refrigerator.

The next day, uncover the mixture and allow it to sit outside the refrigerator for 30 minutes. Then drain the lamb in a colander, reserving the marinade.

Drain the apricots, reserve the water, and set the apricots aside.

Heat the remaining 2 tablespoons of oil in a large, heavy casserole and sauté the onion for 2 minutes. Add the drained lamb and brown it, sautéing for 4 minutes. Add the reserved marinade, apricots, apricot soaking liquid, dates, and chicken stock, and bring the mixture to a boil; allow it to boil for 1 minute.

Reduce the heat to a simmer, cover, and cook gently for 1¼ hours, until the lamb is tender. Remove the cover and continue simmering the lamb until the mixture has thickened slightly.

Serve the lamb over hot, saffron-infused rice and sprinkle the toasted sesame seeds over the top. Serve a small bowl of additional *harissa* on the side.

Yield: 5 to 6 servings

Heat Scale: Medium to Hot, depending on how much harissa *you add at the table*

LAMB AND CAYENNE KEFTA

Keftas are meatballs prepared with ground lamb or beef and a number of herbs and spices. They can be served in a variety of ways: As an addition to stews, as brochettes served hot off the charcoal grill in flat Arab bread, or in pita bread as a sandwich. Although there are many recipes for this dish, the one Moroccan ingredient that seems to remain a constant is fresh mint.

2	teaspoons ground cayenne		1	teaspoon ground ginger
1	pound ground lamb		1	teaspoon ground cardamom
1	medium onion, finely chopped		½	teaspoon ground nutmeg
2	tablespoons chopped fresh mint		½	teaspoon ground cinnamon
1	teaspoon ground cloves		½	teaspoon ground cumin
1	teaspoon ground allspice			Freshly ground black pepper

Combine all the ingredients and allow to sit at room temperature for 1 hour to blend the flavors.

Shape into 1-inch meatballs and thread on skewers. Either slightly flatten them to make into sausage shapes or leave them as balls. Grill the meat over charcoal or under the broiler to the desired doneness.

Yield: 4 servings

Heat Scale: Medium

LAMB TAJINE WITH CHESTNUTS AND CHICKPEAS

This casserole dish is very fragrant when it is simmering. Dried chestnuts are typically used for this recipe in Tunisia, but fresh chestnuts are more readily available in the United States and add even more flavor. With its combination of meat and fruit, this dish is typical of North African cuisine.

2	tablespoons olive oil	½	teaspoon freshly ground black pepper
½	cup chopped celery	1	teaspoon ground cinnamon
1	cup chopped onion	½	teaspoon salt
2	cloves garlic, minced	2	teaspoons crushed red chile
1	pound lamb, cubed	3	cups chestnuts, peeled
½	cup chickpeas, soaked for 12 hours, then drained	¼	cup raisins

Heat the oil in a large, heavy casserole and sauté the celery, onion, and garlic for 2 minutes. Stir in the lamb and sauté it for 1 minute, then add the chickpeas, pepper, and cinnamon. Cover the mixture with water and bring it to a boil. Reduce the heat to a simmer, cover, and cook for 1½ hours.

Add the salt, chile, chestnuts, and raisins, cover, and simmer for 15 to 20 minutes, until the mixture is tender.

Serve with hot cooked rice and chile-dusted sliced tomatoes

Yield: 4 to 6 servings

Heat Scale: Mild

LAMB TAJINE ROAST WITH CAYENNE AND HERBS (T'DLLA)

The use of multiple spices is characteristic of this dish. True to the cooking traditions of the North African desert, the lamb is roasted in an oven. You can eat the hot, roasted lamb by taking a small piece of bread, such as pita bread, and using it to remove some meat, or you may use forks and knives.

1	cup minced onion	1	teaspoon salt
3	cloves garlic, minced	3	teaspoons ground cayenne
1	teaspoon freshly grated ginger	6	tablespoons olive oil
½	teaspoon ground cumin	⅓	cup water
¾	teaspoon ground cinnamon	¼	pound lamb leg or shoulder
⅛	teaspoon crushed saffron threads	⅓	cup butter, melted
		¼	cup chopped cilantro

Preheat the oven to 400 degrees.

Place the onion, garlic, ginger, cumin, cinnamon, saffron, salt, cayenne, olive oil, and water in a small bowl and mix together.

Place the lamb in a heavy ovenproof casserole, deeply pierce the lamb several times, and stuff the onion and spice mixture into as many of the pierced pockets as you can. Pour the remaining mixture over the lamb.

Drizzle 3 tablespoons of the melted butter over the lamb. Add enough water to come one-quarter of the way up the roast. Bring the pan to a boil on top of the stove; when the water boils, cover the pan and place it in the preheated oven for 15 minutes.

Reduce the heat to 350 degrees and cook the lamb for 2 hours, checking to be sure there is some water at the bottom of the pan and drizzling additional butter over the top serveral times as it cooks. The lamb should be so tender that it is falling away from the bone.

An optional finishing touch is to put the lamb under a hot broiler until the top is golden and crisped.

Sprinkle the cilantro over the top of the lamb before serving.

Yield: 5 to 6 servings

Heat Scale: Medium

What Meat to Eat in Africa
When You Run Out of Antelope

- The aardvark is a highly prized delicacy in Zaire and other southern African countries, which might be surprising considering that its diet consists of ants and termites. Its flesh tastes like pork.
- The bone marrow of the giraffe is considered a delicacy in many countries.
- Cane rats, which can weigh up to twenty pounds with a length of two feet, are commonly caught and eaten in Ghana, where they are stewed with *pili-pili* peppers and tomatoes.
- Deer mice—small ruminants also called "mouse deer"—are delicacies in Africa. The largest species, the water cherotain, grows up to twenty-nine pounds.
- Flying foxes, which are really bats, reach three pounds and are hunted with shotguns.
- The pigmy hippopotamus of Liberia and the Ivory Coast has a fatty meat that is considered to be quite a delicacy.

SOSATIES

In this South African recipe, the meat is marinated and then grilled. Many think the recipe had its origins in Malaysia, where Malay *saté*—spiced, grilled meat with hot sauce—is so popular. In Malaysia, it is traditionally grilled over charcoal, and vendors will skewer the meat and grill it right in front of you.

8	dried apricots	½	teaspoon salt
3	tablespoons vegetable oil	3	tablespoons red wine vinegar
1	clove garlic, minced	2	pounds lamb chops or sirloin
3	cups sliced onions	12	to 14 slices bacon
1	teaspoon cayenne powder	3	tablespoons sour cream
5	grape leaves, fresh or bottled		

Wash the apricots, place them in a small saucepan, cover with water, and allow them to soak for 2½ hours. Make sure the apricots are still covered with water, then simmer them for 15 to 20 minutes until they are tender. Allow them to cool slightly, then place them and some of the cooking water in a blender or food processor and purée, adding a little more water if the mixture gets too thick. Set aside.

Heat the oil in a medium skillet and sauté the garlic and the onions for 5 minutes. Add the cayenne, grape leaves, salt, and vinegar. Sauté this mixture for 4 minutes, remove it from the heat, and let it cool slightly.

In a large ceramic bowl, alternately layer the lamb, the bacon, and the apricot mixture. Cover the bowl and marinate overnight in the refrigerator.

Allow the lamb to reach room temperature, then cut it into 1½-inch cubes. Wrap each cube with ½ of a bacon slice, then place them on a skewer. Reserve the extra marinade. Grill the cubes to your liking.

While the meat is grilling, scrape the extra marinade into a small saucepan, add 2 tablespoons of water and the sour cream, and simmer the mixture, taking care not to let it boil.

Serve the meat over hot rice and top with some of the sauce.

Yield: 4 servings

Heat Scale: Mild

BOER LAMB CHOPS MARINATED IN A SPICY SAMBAL

This recipe was influenced by the Cape Malay cuisine, prevalent in South Africa. The word "Boer" in the title is the Dutch word for "farmer." Historically, a Boer in South Africa was part of elite society.

1	cup tomato sauce	8	lamb chops, 1 inch thick
¼	cup cider vinegar	2	tablespoons butter
1½	tablespoons Worcestershire sauce	½	cup beef stock
2	tablespoons Cape Malay *Sambal* (see recipe, p. 20)	½	cup half-and-half cream
2	cups grated onion	3	tablespoons finely minced celery
1	tablespoon dry mustard	½	cup minced leek, white part only
½	teaspoon salt	3	tablespoons minced carrot
¼	teaspoon freshly ground black pepper		

In a shallow-sided ceramic or Pyrex baking dish, stir together the tomato sauce, vinegar, Worcestershire sauce, *sambal,* onion, mustard, salt, and pepper, and then add the lamb chops and turn to coat. Marinate the chops for 1 hour in the refrigerator.

Remove the chops from the marinade (reserving the remaining marinade) and pat the chops dry between paper towels. Heat the butter in a large, heavy skillet and brown the chops quickly to maintain a rare interior. Remove the chops from the pan and place them on paper towels on a warmed plate. Cover the plate with aluminum foil to keep them warm.

Pour the reserved marinade into a small saucepan and add the stock, cream, celery, leek, and carrot, and simmer over a low heat for 10 to 15 minutes, until the vegetables are tender.

Serve the sauce over the rare chops and accompany with a big bowl of steaming hot rice, a green salad, and a big red wine.

Yield: 4 servings

Heat Scale: Mild

A Carnivorous Menu

At the Carnivore Restaurant in Nairobi, Kenya, large cuts of meat are roasted on traditional Masai swords over a huge, visually spectacular charcoal pit that dominates the entrance of the restaurant. The waiters then carry these swords around the restaurant, carving unlimited amounts of prime meats onto sizzling, cast-iron plates in front of the guests. In addition to pork, lamb, beef, and chicken, specialties of the house include venison, impala, Thomson's gazelle, ostrich, giraffe, and crocodile.

BOBOTIE

Bobotie was brought to South Africa in the eighteenth century by Malaysian slaves. There are many variations of this recipe, but the constant ingredient seems to be curry powder. It is traditionally served with plain boiled rice, accompanied by chutney and various condiments, including chopped bananas, sliced green onions, and coconut.

2	slices white bread, 1 inch thick
2	cups milk
2	tablespoons vegetable oil
1½	medium onions, coarsely chopped
2	cloves garlic, minced
1½	tablespoons Malawi Curry Powder (see recipe, p. 14)
1	tablespoon turmeric
1	teaspoon ground ginger
1	teaspoon salt
1	teaspoon freshly ground pepper
2	tablespoons water
1½	pounds ground lamb
1	large tomato, peeled, seeded, and finely chopped
1	large pippin apple, peeled, cored, and chopped
⅓	cup raisins
¼	cup chopped blanched almonds
3	tablespoons mango chutney
1	tablespoon fresh lemon juice
1	tablespoon Worcestershire sauce
1	tablespoon apricot preserves
4	eggs
	Cooked rice

Soak the bread in the milk and set aside.

Heat the oil in a heavy, large skillet over low heat. Add the onions and garlic and cook until golden brown, stirring occasionally, about 15 minutes.

Mix the curry, turmeric, ginger, salt, and pepper into the onion mixture and stir in the water. Simmer the mixture until it thickens slightly, about 2 minutes. Then transfer the mixture to a bowl.

Preheat the oven to 325 degrees.

Add the lamb to the skillet in which the onions were sautéed, and cook the lamb over medium heat until it is no longer pink. Line a bowl with several layers of paper towels and place the cooked lamb on the towels to soak up excess juice. Then add the lamb to the onion mixture and blend in the tomato, apple, raisins, almonds, chutney, lemon juice, Worcestershire sauce, and preserves.

Squeeze the milk from the bread and reserve the milk. Blend the bread into the lamb mixture. Transfer the mixture to a 3-quart soufflé dish.

Beat the reserved milk with the eggs. Pour this over the lamb mixture. Bake until the custard is set and light brown, about 1 hour.

Serve with rice.

Yield: 4 to 6 servings

Heat Scale: Mild

Great Phrases to Know
When Invited to a Swahili Dinner

"Jambo hodi?" (Hello, may I come in?)
"Asante sana." (Many thanks for your hospitality.)
"Kwa heri ya kuonana." (Farewell, until we meet again.)

PINANG-KERRIE

This curry is very popular in South Africa. It is traditionally served dry, which means that the sauce needs to cook until it is very, very thick.

1	tablespoon Malawi Curry Powder (see recipe, p. 14)	1	teaspoon fresh lemon juice or tamarind paste
1	teaspoon turmeric	2	bay leaves
4	cloves garlic, minced	1	pound lamb, cut into 1-inch cubes
½	teaspoon salt	2	tablespoons vegetable oil
2	tablespoons cider vinegar	2	finely sliced onions
1	tablespoon freshly grated ginger	1½	cups chicken stock, or water
1	teaspoon sugar		

In a ceramic bowl, combine the curry powder, turmeric, garlic, salt, vinegar, ginger, sugar, lemon juice, and bay leaves. Add the lamb and toss it gently to cover it with the marinade. Cover the lamb, refrigerate, and allow the mixture to marinate for 2 hours.

Heat the oil in a large, heavy skillet. Add the onions and sauté them for 5 minutes over low heat. Add the lamb and sauté the cubes for 1 minute. Then add the stock or water and simmer the mixture for 40 to 50 minutes, uncovered, or until the meat is tender. Remember, the sauce should be very thick, but be careful to keep just enough moisture in the skillet so that the mixture doesn't burn. Remove the bay leaves before serving.

Serve with a rice dish from Chapter 8.

Yield: 4 to 5 servings

Heat Scale: Mild

LAMB AND MCHICHA, A ONE-DISH MEAL

We thank Richard Sterling for this recipe, which he collected while touring in Kenya. *Mchicha* is a ground-crawling, small-leaf vegetable resembling spinach that is used frequently in local cooking. However, Richard suggests using fresh spinach as a good substitute.

1 pound *mchicha,* or fresh spinach, chopped	1 teaspoon salt Vegetable oil for frying
1 can coconut milk (14 ounces)	1 onion, chopped fine
1 teaspoon ground turmeric	1 can chopped tomatoes (16 ounces)
½ teaspoon ground cloves	
½ teaspoon ground cinnamon	1 bell pepper, stem and seeds removed, finely chopped
1 teaspoon freshly ground cayenne	3 medium potatoes, peeled and diced
1 teaspoon freshly ground black pepper	½ pound coarsely ground lamb

Combine the spinach, coconut milk, turmeric, cloves, cinnamon, cayenne, black pepper, and salt, and simmer 5 minutes. Set aside.

Sauté the onion, tomatoes, and bell pepper in a little oil until the onion is soft and translucent, then remove them from the pan. Add more oil to the pan and fry the potatoes, then drain and set aside.

Place the meat in a large pot with enough water to cover it, and simmer until the meat is tender. Add all the other ingredients to the pot and simmer for an additional 20 minutes.

Serve with a green salad and sliced oranges.

Yield: 4 servings

Heat Scale: Medium

LEG OF LAMB IN HOT SAUCE (YEBEG INFILLE)

This Ethiopian recipe is a great dish to serve at a dinner party because guests can eat with their fingers! The meat can be scooped up with *Injera* Bread (see recipe, p. 217), and then dipped into the spicy sauce. The lamb strips can be boiled first, although traditionally they are served raw.

1	leg of lamb	2	cups water
1	tablespoon vegetable oil	½	teaspoon freshly minced ginger
1	cup chopped onion	¼	teaspoon freshly ground white pepper
¾	cup *Berbere* Paste (see recipe, p. 25)	½	teaspoon salt
1	cup Ethiopian Curried Butter (see recipe, p. 37)	1	cup dry red wine
1	clove garlic, minced	½	teaspoon ground cardamom

Have your butcher cut the lamb into thin strips, leaving it attached to the bone. If you are serving it raw, proceed to make the sauce. If you are cooking the meat, place it in a very large casserole or stock pot, cover with water, bring the water to a boil, reduce heat, and simmer covered until the meat is very tender. Remove the leg from the pot and drain it thoroughly.

Heat the oil in a large skillet. Add the onion and sauté until it is slightly brown, about 5 minutes, stirring. Add the *berbere,* butter, and garlic, and stir constantly for 3 minutes.

Stir in the 2 cups of water and the ginger, pepper, salt, wine, and cardamom, and simmer for 20 minutes, stirring occasionally.

Serve the sauce with the lamb and *Injera* Bread (see recipe, p. 217).

Yield: 6 to 8 servings

Heat Scale: Medium

JOLLOF RICE

One-dish dinners are beloved in Africa, and this rice dish is popular in Ghana, Sierra Leone, Gambia, and all of West Africa. It is served with many kinds of meats, depending on what's available, and it can also be served without any meat at all. The name is undoubtedly derived from an ancient tribe called the "Wolofs."

3	tablespoons peanut oil	2	teaspoons ground ginger
2	pounds chicken, cubed	2	bay leaves
½	pound beef, cut into 1½-inch cubes	2	cups beef stock
2	cups chopped onion	½	pound smoked ham, cut in 1½-inch cubes
2½	cups peeled, deseeded, chopped tomatoes	1	small cabbage, cut into small wedges
5	green New Mexican chiles, roasted, peeled, seeds and stems removed, and chopped	3	tablespoons tomato paste
		2	cups long-grain rice
3	teaspoons ground cayenne	4	cups water

Heat the oil in a large, heavy casserole. Add the chicken and sauté until browned. Then add the beef and onion, and sauté for 2 minutes.

Stir in the tomatoes, chiles, cayenne, ginger, and bay leaves. Simmer the mixture for 5 minutes, then add the stock. Bring the mixture to a boil, reduce the heat, cover, and simmer for 1 hour.

Add the ham and cabbage and simmer for an additional 15 minutes.

Mix the tomato paste with the rice, add the rice to the simmering meat, and stir in 4 cups of water. Bring the mixture to a boil, cover, reduce the heat to a simmer, and cook for 15 to 20 minutes, until the rice is done. Allow the dish to sit, covered, for 15 minutes before serving.

Yield: 8 servings

Heat Scale: Medium

MARINATED AND GRILLED ROUND STEAK (TSITSINGA)

Tsitsinga requires some marinating, which helps to flavor and tenderize the meat. The original version of this dish requires roasted corn flour—*ablemanu*. Since *ablemanu* is difficult to find, we suggest that you substitute oven-toasted corn meal.

1	cup vegetable oil		1	piece fresh ginger (2 inches)
2	tablespoons red wine vinegar		3	jalapeño chiles, seeds and stems removed
1	teaspoon salt			
1	pound round steak, cut into 1-inch cubes		1	tomato, peeled
½	cup sliced onion		½	cup oven-toasted corn meal

In a flat ceramic dish, mix together ½ cup of the oil, the vinegar, and the salt. Add the meat and toss to coat. Marinate in the refrigerator for at least 1 hour.

Place the onion, ginger, chiles, and tomato in a blender and purée. Scoop the purée into a small bowl and set aside.

Place the meat on skewers and grill it until it is half done, approximately 5 minutes. Then remove the meat from the skewers and toss it in the vegetable purée to thoroughly coat it. Re-skewer the meat, sprinkle it with the corn meal, drizzle it with the remaining oil, and grill until it is done. Serve immediately.

Serve this dish with hot cooked rice, a salad, and a sauce such as Nigerian Fried Red Pepper Sauce (*Ata Dindin*), p. 32.

Yield: 4 to 5 servings

Heat Scale: Medium

BEEF BERBERE (YESIGA T'IBS)

This dish is very common in Ethiopia. The ingredients listed here are the ones used most frequently, but some cooks will add additional herbs, spices, and vegetables to give it a special touch. Part of the rich flavor of this dish comes from caramelizing the onions.

1½ cups chopped onion	1½ pounds beef, cut into 1-inch cubes
⅔ cup Ethiopian Curried Butter (see recipe, p. 37)	¼ teaspoon ground cardamom
1 cup *Berbere* Paste (see recipe, p. 25)	½ teaspoon salt
	1 clove garlic, minced
¾ cup dry red wine	¼ teaspoon freshly ground black pepper

Heat a medium-sized heavy skillet, add the onions and the curried butter, and, over a very low heat, sauté them slowly until they are brownish in color. Stir occasionally to make sure they don't burn.

Add the *berbere* and wine, and simmer the mixture for 2 minutes. Then add the beef, cardamom, salt, garlic, and pepper. Cover and simmer for 20 to 30 minutes, until the meat is tender.

This dish is usually served with *Injera* Bread (see recipe, p. 217).

Yield: 4 to 6 servings

Heat Scale: Medium Hot

ETHIOPIAN GROUND BEEF WITH PEPPERS (RETFO)

One constant factor in Ethiopian cooking is the use of red hot chiles, and this recipe is no exception. It combines ease of preparation and minimal cooking time—quick, easy, spicy fast food!

1½ pounds lean ground beef	½ teaspoon salt
1 tablespoon vegetable oil	¼ teaspoon freshly ground black pepper
1 cup chopped onion	
½ cup chopped bell pepper	½ cup chopped tomato, or ¼ cup tomato sauce (optional)
2 cloves garlic, minced	
2 dried *piri-piri* or *piquin* chiles, seeds and stems removed, coarsely crushed	

Sauté the beef in a large skillet until all of the pink is gone. Place the meat in a sieve lined with paper towels to absorb the excess grease.

Wipe out the skillet, add the oil, and sauté the onion, bell pepper, and garlic until the onion is soft, about 2 or 3 minutes.

Add the drained beef, chiles, salt, pepper, and tomatoes; cover and sauté for 6 minutes.

Serve over hot cooked rice with a cucumber salad on the side.

Yield: 6 servings

Heat Scale: Medium

PEPPER-PEANUT BEEF KEBABS

The combination of two ingredients native to the tropics—peppers and peanuts—is a natural in these kebabs. This recipe is from our good friend, Jeffrey Gerlach, who was in Nigeria with the Peace Corps. In Nigeria, they are served hot off the grill, and Jeff says they are sold on every street corner; they are very, very, spicy, but so delicious. Jeff, and his wife, Nancy, now make these in Albuquerque, and everyone sits around the picnic table and yells for more! Warning: These are extremely addictive.

1½ pounds beef, cut in 1½- to 2-inch cubes

12 ounces beer

1½ cups crushed peanuts

⅔ cup crushed dried red New Mexican chile, seeds included

Marinate the beef in the beer for 3 to 4 hours.

Roll the beef cubes in a mixture of the peanuts and chile until they are completely covered. Put the cubes on skewers and grill over charcoal until done.

Serve over hot rice and with a fruit salad.

Yield: 4 to 6 servings

Heat Scale: Hot

129

WEST AFRICAN BEEF KEBABS (SUYA)

This traditional recipe sells well all over West Africa, even in the remote corners of all the countries. It is very hot and spicy. This recipe is a little more complicated than Pepper-Peanut Beef Kebabs (see recipe, p. 129) and has a slightly different taste, but it is equally delicious.

3 pounds beef sirloin, cut into 1-inch cubes	2 pounds calves' liver, cut into 1½-inch cubes
2 tablespoons fresh lemon juice	2 teaspoons freshly grated ginger
¼ cup grated onion	½ teaspoon salt
1 clove garlic, minced	⅓ cup melted butter
2 crushed hot red *piri-piri* or *piquin* chiles, or 2 teaspoons cayenne	1½ cups roasted peanuts, finely ground

Place the cubed beef in a ceramic bowl and toss with the lemon juice, onion, garlic, and chiles. Cover the mixture and refrigerate overnight.

In another ceramic bowl, mix together the liver, ginger, and salt; cover and marinate in the refrigerator overnight.

Place the beef and liver, alternating, on skewers, brush with the melted butter, roll the skewers in the crushed peanuts, and broil the meat for about 6 minutes, turning once.

Variation: The meats can also be alternated with parboiled pearl onions, tomatoes, and/or mushrooms.

Yield: 6 to 8 servings
Heat Scale: Medium

ROMAZAVA

According to Judith Ritter, this is the "national dish" of Madagascar. The dish is easy to make, with ingredients that are easily found in every supermarket. Since the heat comes from the sauce, each diner can adjust the amount used as preferred.

2   teaspoons cooking oil
1   pound beef shank, cut into small cubes
½   medium onion, chopped
2   cloves garlic, minced
1   teaspoon minced fresh ginger
2   ripe tomatoes, chopped
1   cup beef broth

1   bunch watercress, chopped
½   pound fresh spinach, chopped
½   pound Chinese cabbage, chopped
Salt and pepper to taste
Madagascar Sauce Dynamite (see recipe, p. 21)

In a medium-sized, heavy skillet, heat the oil and sauté the beef, onion, garlic, and ginger. Add the tomatoes and broth, cover, and cook over low heat, 45 minutes to 1 hour.

Add the watercress, spinach, and cabbage, and cook for 10 minutes over low heat. Add salt and pepper to taste.

Serve the *Romazava* over hot cooked rice or a simple pilau, accompanied by the Madagascar Sauce Dynamite. For a salad, serve cucumbers marinated in vinegar.

Yield: 4 servings

Heat Scale: Varies, depending on how much Madagascar Sauce Dynamite one adds

PAPAYA GINGER BEEF WITH PIRI-PIRIS

We thank our friend in Africa, Michelle Cox of Malindi, Kenya, for this terrific recipe. She likes this recipe in particular because fresh papaya served with lime juice on the top is one of her favorites. is Papaya is also a natural meat tenderizer; just place the fresh slices on both sides of the piece of meat you wish to tenderize, and leave it at room temperature for 1 hour. It's good for digestion. Medicinally, it's applied to jellyfish stings to draw out the toxins.

1	pound sirloin	2	cups beef stock
1	barely ripe papaya	½	teaspoon salt
2	cups ice water	¼	teaspoon freshly ground black pepper
1	tablespoon salt		
2	tablespoons vegetable oil	1	tablespoon cornstarch
1	onion, thinly sliced	½	cup water
2	tablespoons crushed fresh ginger	1	teaspoon soy sauce
3	green *piri-piri* chiles, or jalapeños, seeds and stems removed, sliced very thin		

Place the beef in the freezer for 30 minutes to facilitate slicing.

Deseed the papaya, peel it, and cut it into 1-inch cubes. Add the salt to the ice water, and place the papaya cubes in the ice water; soak the cubes for 1 hour. Rinse the cubes well in cold water and drain.

Remove the beef from the freezer, slice it as thinly as possible, and set it aside.

Heat the oil in a large, heavy skillet and sauté the onion until golden. Then add the beef, ginger, chiles, and papaya. Stir-fry for a few minutes, taking care not to break the papaya pieces. Add the stock, salt, and pepper, and bring to a boil.

Combine the cornstarch with the ½ cup of water and the soy sauce. Add this mixture to the meat and simmer until the mixture has thickened.

Serve the beef hot with freshly cooked rice.

Yield: 4 servings

Heat Scale: Medium

Cattle As Pets

"East Africa is another region well known for its petlike treatment of animals that are good to eat. It is the men rather than the women who tend cattle and who grow more intimately attached to these animals. They talk and sing about their oxen and cows, groom them, and decorate them with tassels, wooden beads, and bells. Among the Dinka, husbands and wives sleep apart; the husbands sleeps inside his cattle house, amid his cattle, while his wives and children sleep in separate huts nearby. Like most pastoralists, the cattle lovers derive the principal portions of their animal food from milk and milk products. But they have a well-developed taste for beef, which they indulge upon the natural death of an older animal and at feasts commemorating important events such as funerals, marriages, and the change of seasons."

Marvin Harris

SPICY VEAL CASSEROLE WITH TOMATO TOPPING (HURIS HILIB)

This recipe is basically a Somalian meat loaf with chiles, even though it contains chopped veal instead of ground beef.

1	cup quartered potatoes	¼	teaspoon freshly ground white or black pepper
1	bell pepper, seeded and sliced		
2	tablespoons vegetable oil	3	fresh jalapeño chiles, stems and seeds removed, finely chopped
¾	cup chopped onion		
1	pound veal, cut into ¼-inch cubes	1½	teaspoons basil
1	clove garlic, minced	2	large fresh tomatoes, peeled and sliced

Fill a large saucepan with water, bring to a boil, and add the potatoes and the bell pepper. Boil lightly for 10 minutes, then drain. When cooled, place the potatoes and bell pepper in a food processor and grind coarsely. Set the mixture aside.

Heat the oil in a large skillet and sauté the onion and the veal for 12 to 15 minutes, until the meat has browned. Stir in the garlic, pepper, chiles, and basil. Add the reserved potato mixture and stir it into the sautéed meat.

Preheat the oven to 325 degrees.

Lightly oil a small 1- or 1½-quart ovenproof casserole and place half the sliced tomatoes on the bottom; cover with the meat mixture, and place the remaining tomatoes on the top. Cover with a lid or with aluminum foil and bake for 20 minutes.

Serve with a green salad and warm, crusty bread.

Yield: 4 servings

Heat Scale: Medium

134

The Ubiquitous African Chicken

In Africa, chicken has always been perceived as something of a delicacy. It is said that in even the most impoverished households, a good housewife will always have at least one chicken in her back yard, specially reared, to prepare when an important guest arrives unexpectedly. You might say they had the original free-range chicken!

While modern conveniences such as frozen poultry from the grocery store have probably precluded some Africans from raising fowl, by tradition—and in rural areas by necessity—African cooks continue to perform magic with chicken and the ingredients that make up fine foods around the world: Minimally processed grains, fresh and exotic fruits and vegetables, fresh-cut herbs, and hand-ground spices.

It is the spice that we will focus on in this chapter—how this gold of ancient times, traded in Zanzibar, Marrakech, and Timbuktu, mingles with poultry to create incredible cuisine.

We begin our culinary adventure in Kenya with two recipes that feature coconut: Sidi's Tamarind and Coconut Chicken (p. 138) and Hyderabad Chicken Curry (p. 140). We hope you'll try using fresh coconut in these recipes; although it is a bit more trouble, the special taste is well worth the time.

Our next four recipes are *tajines,* probably Morocco's most ubiquitous dish. From the Hot *Tajine* of Chicken with Lemons and Olives (p. 139) to Chicken with Spiced Almonds (p. 142), *Tajine Tafarout* (p. 143), and Cayenne Chicken *Tajine* Smothered in a Spicy Eggplant Purée (p. 144), no matter how often you eat it, this dish is almost impossible to tire of, as each chef puts a personal stamp on his or her creation.

Chicken *Doro We't* (p. 147) is the most popular Ethiopian dish served on special occasions. You might like to serve it, or perhaps the Chicken Dipped in Hot Sauce (p. 148), with a side of yogurt and your favorite bread from Chapter 8.

If you're up for a heat treat, we suggest the Five-Chile Chicken (p. 149). However, the Moroccan Chicken with Preserved Lemons (p. 150), Chicken with Chickpeas, Lemon, and Parsley (p. 152), and Moroccan Pigeon Pie (p. 154) provide a more aromatic and less heated taste of Africa.

The tiny West African country of Ghana is the largest exporter of cocoa in the world. It is also the birthplace of *Palaver* Chicken (p. 151). We introduce a taste of India with our next two fares, Chicken *Tikka* (p. 156) and East African Spiced and Roasted Chicken (p. 158).

Our last three recipes offer diverse choices likely to please any pepper-loving palate. Chicken with Spinach and Yogurt (p. 157), *Yassa au Poulet* (p. 160), and Zanzibar Duck (p. 161) are highly spiced and perfect for both everyday and special-occasion meals.

SIDI'S TAMARIND AND COCONUT CHICKEN

This is an authentic home recipe, shared by the wife of the food-and-beverage manager of the Driftwood Beach Club in Malindi, Kenya. Recipe collector Michelle Cox says, "Although he spends his whole life around food, he never tires of being served this dish when he gets away from the hotel kitchen."

8	pieces of chicken (preferably legs and thighs)
	Oil for browning
1	medium onion, chopped
1	medium tomato, chopped
2	cloves garlic, chopped
2	to 3 Kenya chiles, seeds and stems removed, chopped fine, or fresh red jalapeños
1	heaping teaspoon turmeric powder
	Salt and pepper to taste
2	cups coconut milk
1	cup lime juice

In a frying pan, brown chicken on all sides in oil. Remove chicken and set aside.

To the pan, add onion, tomato, garlic, chiles, turmeric, and salt and pepper, frying until the onion is browned. Return chicken to the pan. Pour over the coconut milk and lime juice. Simmer over low heat for 30 minutes, until the chicken is cooked through.

Serve with rice.

Yield: 4 servings

Heat Scale: Hot

HOT TAJINE OF CHICKEN WITH LEMONS AND OLIVES

These stews are slowly simmered for long periods of time so that the meat literally falls off the bone. They are then placed in the center of the room and everyone eats out of the communal bowl by using small pieces of unleavened bread to pick up the stew. Rosemary Ann Ogilvie collected this *tajine* for us in Morocco.

1	chicken fryer (3 pounds), cut in serving pieces	1	large onion, thinly sliced
3	tablespoons vegetable oil	1	tomato, peeled and diced
1	teaspoon ground ginger	6	cloves garlic, minced
1	teaspoon ground New Mexican red chile		Juice of one lemon
½	teaspoon ground turmeric	2	cups water
¼	teaspoon ground cumin	2	lemons, quartered
½	cup chopped fresh parsley	1	jar (14 ounces) green olives (not stuffed), drained

In a large skillet, quickly brown the chicken in the oil. Add the ginger, chile, turmeric, cumin, parsley, onion, tomato, garlic, lemon juice, and water. Bring to a boil, then reduce the heat and simmer, covered, until the chicken is tender, about 1½ hours, turning the chicken frequently.

Remove the chicken from the sauce and keep it warm. When ready to serve, return the chicken to the pan, add the lemon quarters and the olives, and simmer for 10 minutes.

Serve on a plate or in a traditionally made *tajine* with flat pita-type bread.

Yield: 4 servings

Heat Scale: Mild

HYDERABAD CHICKEN CURRY

From Kenya comes this imported curry, originating in India, which is the way things work in immigrant-happy Africa. To spice it up even further, substitute jalapeños for the New Mexican chiles.

¼	teaspoon saffron threads	4	whole cloves
1	tablespoon chicken stock	1	tablespoon caraway seed
1	cup plain yogurt	1	cinnamon stick (¾ inches), broken into small pieces
3	medium cloves garlic, minced		
2	teaspoons chopped fresh ginger	1¼	teaspoons turmeric
		1	teaspoon salt
1	chicken (3½ pounds) cut into 6 pieces and patted dry	3	tablespoons ghee, or vegetable oil
3	New Mexican chiles, roasted, peeled, seeds and stems removed, and chopped (about 6 ounces total)	2	medium onions, thinly sliced
		3	tablespoons grated coconut
		1	cup chicken stock
10	cardamom pods, skinned, seeds removed and reserved	1	tablespoon fresh lemon juice
			Cilantro (coriander) leaves for garnish
6	black peppercorns		

Crush the saffron and dissolve it in the chicken stock. Combine the yogurt, garlic, ginger, and dissolved saffron in a large bowl. Add the chicken, and marinate at room temperature for 2 hours, turning occasionally.

Meanwhile, char the chiles over a gas flame or under a broiler until the skins blister and blacken. Place in a plastic bag. Seal tightly and let steam for 10 minutes. Peel off the skins and discard the seeds. Transfer the chiles to a food processor or blender and purée.

In a heavy, medium-sized skillet on medium heat, cook the cardamom pods and seeds, peppercorns, cloves, caraway seed, and cinnamon until aromatic, 6 to 7 minutes. Transfer to a small bowl and let cool. Mix to a powder in a spice grinder or blender. Return the mixture to a small bowl and stir in the chile purée, turmeric, and salt.

Melt the ghee (or heat the oil) in heavy, large skillet over medium-low heat. Add the onions and stir until golden, 5 to 7 minutes. Blend in the spice mixture and stir for 2 minutes. Add the chicken pieces with their marinade and the grated coconut. Increase the heat to medium-high and bring to a boil. Stir in the stock and return to a boil. Reduce the heat to low and simmer until the chicken is tender, about 20 minutes for white meat and 30 minutes for dark, turning the pieces once.

Transfer the chicken to a platter. Add the lemon juice to the sauce and pour over the top. Garnish with cilantro and serve.

This recipe is best served with freshly cooked *basmati* rice. *Basmati* is a delicate rice from the Indian Continent and may be either white or brown.

Yield: 4 servings

Heat Scale: Medium

A Fiery Remedy

"West Africans are extremely fond of highly seasoned food. Most often the heat is generated by red peppers, used in quantities hard to believe. A home economics teacher in Lagos gave me her recipe for Pepper Chicken, which calls for four large red peppers or one tablespoon of cayenne. Red peppers have medicinal uses in West Africa, too. They are widely regarded as a cold remedy, eaten whole and uncooked, like an apple. This undoubtedly flushes out all eight sinus cavities as well as the tear ducts."

Harva Hachten

CHICKEN WITH SPICED ALMONDS (POULET AU GNEMBOUE)

This recipe is a simple North African *tajine,* intensely flavored with almonds and cayenne.

1	cup almonds	1	clove garlic
1¾	cups water	3	scallions or green onions, thinly sliced
2	teaspoons cayenne pepper		
¼	teaspoon black pepper	1	chicken (2½ pounds), cut for frying
1	teaspoon salt		

Pulverize the nuts with a mortar and pestle, and mix with the water. Pour the mixture into a 12-inch skillet or saucepan. Stir in the peppers, salt, garlic, and onions; mix ingredients well.

Place the pieces of chicken in the nut mixture; cover and cook over very low heat for 1½ hours. Check often; stir and add water if needed.

Serve over couscous.

Yield: 4 to 6 servings

Heat Scale: Hot

TAJINE TAFAROUT

This *tajine* honors the flowering of the almond trees and comes from Tafarout, Morocco. It is often served at a wedding feast.

1	chicken (3 to 4 pounds), cut in serving pieces	½	teaspoon ground cinnamon
¼	cup extra-virgin olive oil	¼	teaspoon ground turmeric
1	large onion, finely sliced	2	cups water
4	teaspoons ground cayenne	1	cup dried apricot halves, soaked in water until soft
1	teaspoon ground ginger	1	cup whole, blanched almonds
1	teaspoon ground coriander	2	tablespoons butter or margarine
½	teaspoon ground cumin		

Brown the chicken in the olive oil; when evenly browned, remove. Pour off all but a few tablespoons of the oil.

Add the onion and sauté until browned. Add the spices and sauté for 2 minutes. Add the water and bring to a boil.

Reduce the heat, add the chicken pieces and apricots, and simmer for 30 minutes, turning the chicken frequently, until the chicken is very tender and starts to fall from the bone. Add more water if necessary.

Brown the almonds in the butter, remove, and drain.

To serve, arrange the chicken on a platter, top with the sauce, and garnish with the almonds. Serve with a carrot salad, couscous, and pita bread.

Yield: 4 servings

Heat Scale: Hot

CAYENNE CHICKEN TAJINE SMOTHERED IN A SPICY EGGPLANT PURÉE (TAJINE MDERBEL)

Here chicken simmers in a sauce of garlic, ginger, saffron, and black pepper until it is tender. Then the chicken is piled in the center of a dish and topped with a thick, intensely flavored sauce of fried eggplant, tomatoes, and spices.

2	pounds eggplant		A pinch of sugar
2	tablespoons plus 2 teaspoons coarse (kosher) salt		A pinch of salt plus additional to taste
	Olive oil or corn oil, for shallow frying	2	tablespoons lemon juice, plus additional to taste
3	medium cloves garlic, crushed	1	tablespoon cider vinegar
¼	cup chopped Italian flat-leaf parsley	1	chicken (about 4 pounds), cut into 8 pieces
¼	cup chopped fresh coriander	1¼	teaspoons ground ginger
1	teaspoon sweet paprika		A pinch of powdered saffron
¼	teaspoon ground cumin	¼	teaspoon finely ground black pepper, plus additional to taste
1	teaspoon cayenne		
2	large tomatoes, peeled, seeded and chopped (about 2 cups)	½	cup grated onion (2 small onions)

Trim off the top and bottom from each eggplant. With a vegetable peeler, remove 3 to 4 thin vertical strips of skin from each vegetable, leaving the eggplants striped, then cut crosswise into ½-inch slices. Sprinkle the eggplant with 2 tablespoons of the salt and let drain in a non-aluminum colander for at least 2 hours, or preferably overnight.

Rinse and drain the eggplant; pat dry with paper towels.

Heat ¼ inch of oil in a large, heavy skillet over high heat. Fry the eggplant slices in batches until golden brown on both sides, about 4 minutes. Drain on paper towels; place on a cutting board. Strain the oil and reserve.

With a potato masher, crush the eggplant with 1 of the garlic cloves, 2 tablespoons each of the parsley and coriander, and the paprika, cumin, and cayenne.

Return 3 tablespoons of the reserved oil to the skillet and reheat. Add the tomatoes, 1 teaspoon of the salt, and the sugar. Cook over moderately high heat, stirring frequently, until most of the moisture evaporates, about 5 minutes.

Add the mashed eggplant to the tomatoes in the skillet and cook over very low heat, stirring frequently, until most of the moisture evaporates and the mixture is very thick, about 20 minutes.

Remove from the heat and stir in the lemon juice and vinegar. (The recipe can be prepared to this point up to 3 days in advance.)

Wash the chicken; pat dry. In a mortar, pound the remaining garlic with the remaining teaspoon of salt. Blend in the ginger, saffron, and black pepper. Using a whisk, slowly stir in 2 tablespoons of the reserved oil and the hot water.

In a large flameproof casserole or deep skillet, toss the chicken with the garlic-spice mixture to coat each piece. Cover and cook over low heat for 5 minutes. Add the onion, the remaining parsley and coriander, and enough water to just cover, about 2½ cups. Bring to a boil, reduce the heat to moderate, cover and simmer for 1 hour or until the chicken begins to fall off the bone.

Preheat the oven to 400 degrees.

Remove the chicken to a serving dish and cover to keep moist. Skim off most of the fat, then continue cooking the pan juices uncovered over moderate heat until reduced to 1½ cups, about 15 minutes.

Mix half the pan juices with the eggplant purée and adjust the seasoning, adding salt, black pepper, and lemon juice to taste.

Place the chicken in a small heat-proof serving bowl. Pile the eggplant mixture on top, forming a pyramid. Surround with the remaining sauce. Cover loosely with foil and reheat for 10 minutes in the oven just before serving.

Garnish the purée with thin slices of lemon and sprigs of coriander if desired.

Yield: 4 to 6 servings

Heat Scale: Medium

What Poultry to Eat in Africa
When You Run Out of Chicken

- The largest flying bird by weight is the *kori,* a type of bustard. It is considered a delicious treat in Africa, and can weigh up to fifty pounds.
- The tongue of the African flamingo was considered to be quite a delicacy in ancient Rome.
- Guinea fowl, called the Carthaginian Hen by the Romans, is extremely tasty. We have had it exquisitely prepared at Jeffrey's Restaurant in Austin, Texas.
- Ostrich meat, which is now being commercially grown in North America, looks and tastes like beef but is lower in fat and cholesterol than chicken.

CHICKEN DORO WE'T

Also spelled *"wa't,"* *doro we't* or chicken stew is the most well-known of the "national dishes" of Ethiopia. This dish is served over *Injera* Bread (see recipe, p. 217). The serving dish is a brightly colored woven straw basket, three feet high, that is placed in the center of the room. Everyone sits around it and eats the "wa't" with their fingers.

1 chicken (3 pounds) cut into small pieces
3 tablespoons lemon juice
1 large onion, chopped
2 cloves garlic, chopped
2 tablespoons butter or margarine
2 teaspoons ground ginger
1 teaspoon ground black pepper

¼ teaspoon ground cardamom
¼ teaspoon ground nutmeg
¼ cup *Berbere* Paste (see recipe, p. 25)
2 tablespoons paprika
  Water as needed
4 hard-cooked eggs, peeled, left whole

Remove the skin and score the chicken so the sauce will penetrate the meat. Rub the chicken with the lemon juice and let it marinate for 30 minutes at room temperature.

Sauté the onion and garlic in the butter until browned. Add the spices, *berbere,* and paprika, and cook for 2 to 3 minutes.

Add the chicken to the pan and toss to coat. Stir in enough water to form a thick sauce. Bring to a boil, reduce the heat, cover, and simmer for 30 minutes or until the meat starts to fall off the bone.

Using a fork, poke holes all over the eggs, then add them to the stew. Cover again and simmer for an additional 15 minutes.

Yield: 4 servings

Heat Scale: Hot

CHICKEN DIPPED IN HOT SAUCE (YEDORO INFILLE)

This recipe hails from Ethiopia, known as the land of thirteen months of sunshine. *Yedoro Infille* is best eaten with *Injera* Bread (see recipe, p. 217), and the sauce mixed with some yogurt.

1	whole chicken		Salt to taste
1	cup plus ¼ cup red onions, chopped	1	tablespoon ginger
1	cup butter	1	tablespoon chopped garlic
2	teaspoons cayenne pepper	¼	teaspoon black pepper
2	cups water	¼	cup *Berbere* Paste (see recipe, p. 25)

Skin chicken and cut into the usual pieces (leg, thigh, breast, etc.). Set aside the smaller pieces (neck, wings, etc.). With the larger pieces, leave the meat attached to the bones, cut the chicken into strips, and set aside.

In a medium pan, brown 1 cup of the onions with the butter, add the cayenne pepper, and stir gently. Add 1 cup of the water and stir well.

Add the large chicken pieces to the cooked onions. Stir in the salt, ginger, garlic, and black pepper. Cook for 20 to 30 minutes, adding the remaining water as needed.

In another pan, boil the rest of the small pieces of chicken with the remaining uncooked onion for 15 minutes. Remove the smaller chicken parts from the water and dip them into the prepared *Berbere* sauce.

Serve hot.

Yield: 6 servings

Heat Scale: Medium

FIVE-CHILE CHICKEN

This West African dish is popular in Nigeria, and is very hot. However, feel free to adjust the heat level up or down to your taste. This recipe is a perfect choice when introducing African Cuisine to guests, as it is spicy, and the traditional tastes of okra and ginger really shine through.

½ cup lemon juice

1 fryer chicken (3 pounds)

½ cup water

2 tablespoons vegetable oil (palm oil is traditional)

2 tomatoes, skinned and sieved or crushed

5 green chiles, such as jalapeño, seeds and stems removed, minced

1 piece ginger root (½ inch), grated

½ pound okra, ends cut off, sliced

2 cups chicken stock

Salt and pepper to taste

Mix the lemon juice with the water. Remove the skin and fat from the chicken, cut it up, and acidulate it in the lemon-water solution; this is the African way of combating bacteria.

While the chicken is acidulating, heat half the vegetable oil in a skillet and sauté the sieved tomatoes, chiles, grated ginger root, and okra for about 8 minutes. Remove the sautéed ingredients from the skillet and set aside.

Drain and dry the chicken with paper towels, then brown them in the skillet with the remaining vegetable oil. Add the stock and sautéed ingredients, cover, and simmer for about 40 to 60 minutes. Taste for seasoning adjustment.

Serve over your favorite starch: Dumplings, stiff cornmeal mush, or rice.

Yield: 4 servings

Heat Scale: Hot

MOROCCAN CHICKEN WITH PRESERVED LEMONS

This is one of the spicier *tajines* we have encountered. The flavor combinations of the preserved lemons, olives, and chiles is truly unique. For less sodium, use ripe olives instead of calamatas.

2	tablespoons olive oil	½	teaspoon black pepper
3	pounds chicken thighs, skinned and rinsed	1	cup water
1	large (about ½ pound) onion, chopped	½	cup calamata olives (optional)
2	teaspoons hot paprika	10	Moroccan preserved lemon quarters (available in ethnic markets)
1	teaspoon ground ginger	¼	cup finely chopped fresh cilantro
½	teaspoon ground turmeric		
1	tablespoon cayenne		

Pour the oil into a 10- to 12-inch frying pan over medium-high heat. Add the chicken and turn often to brown on all sides, about 15 minutes. Lift out the chicken and set it aside.

Remove all but 1 tablespoon of oil from pan. Add the onion and stir often over medium-high heat until tinged with brown, about 5 minutes. Stir in paprika, ginger, turmeric, cayenne, and pepper. Add the cup of water, the chicken, the olives, and 6 of the preserved lemons and their liquid.

Cover the pan and simmer, turning the chicken once, until the meat is no longer pink at the bone (cut to test), 20 to 25 minutes. Skim the liquid and discard the fat. Transfer the chicken and sauce to a wide bowl.

Garnish the chicken with the remaining lemon wedges and cilantro. Serve with rice or couscous.

Yield: 4 servings

Heat Scale: Hot

PALAVER CHICKEN

This is a variation of the popular *Palaver* Sauce from Ghana (see recipe, p. 30), which was originally made from fish. In Africa, a sauce is sometimes a stew. This version is from Sierra Leone, where peanut butter is often added.

1½ pounds skinless, boneless chicken breasts

2 cloves garlic, crushed
Salt and freshly ground black pepper

2 tablespoons butter or margarine

2 tablespoons vegetable oil (palm oil is traditional)

1 onion, finely chopped

4 tomatoes, peeled and chopped

2 tablespoons peanut butter

2½ cups chicken stock or water

1 thyme sprig, or 1 teaspoon dried thyme

8 ounces frozen leaf spinach, defrosted and chopped

2 green chiles, such as jalapeños, seeds and stems removed, chopped

Cut the chicken breasts into thin slices and place them in a bowl. Stir in the garlic and a little salt and pepper. Melt the butter or margarine in a large frying pan and fry the chicken over moderate heat, turning once or twice to brown evenly. Using a slotted spoon, transfer the chicken to a plate and set aside.

Heat the oil in a large saucepan and fry the onion and tomatoes over high heat for 5 minutes or until soft. Reduce the heat, add the peanut butter and half the stock, and blend together well.

Cook for 4 to 5 minutes, stirring constantly to keep the peanut butter from burning, then add the remaining stock, the thyme, spinach, and chiles, and salt and pepper to taste. Stir in the chicken slices and cook over moderate heat for about 10 to 15 minutes, or until the chicken is cooked through.

Pour into a warmed serving dish and serve with boiled yams or rice.

Yield: 4 to 6 servings

Heat Scale: Medium

CHICKEN WITH CHICKPEAS, LEMON, AND PARSLEY

In this Algerian dish, the sauce is thickened with grated onion, parsley, and cilantro, and luxuriously flavored with saffron and lemon juice.

2 cloves garlic, crushed	3 ounces green onions, white part only, chopped
Salt	1 cinnamon stick
½ teaspoon ground ginger	6 ounces chickpeas, soaked overnight
½ teaspoon cayenne	
A pinch of saffron threads	1 small red onion, finely chopped
¼ cup unsalted butter, softened	Lemon juice
1 chicken (3¼ pounds)	
1 small bunch mixed parsley and cilantro, finely chopped	

Crush the garlic with a pinch of salt, then mix it with the ginger, cayenne, and saffron in a small bowl. Blend in half the butter then rub the mixture over the chicken. Put the chicken in a large dish, cover it with plastic, and refrigerate overnight.

The next day, put the chicken and any juices left in the dish in a saucepan that will just fit the chicken. Add half the herbs, the green onions, the cinnamon stick, the chickpeas, and enough water to just cover the chicken. Heat to a simmering point, then cook gently for about 1¼ to 1½ hours or until tender, turning the chicken a couple of times.

Meanwhile, melt the remaining butter in a small pan, then add the red onion and cook until softened, without allowing it to color.

Lift the chicken from its pan, draining the liquid from the cavity back into the pan, and cover tightly with foil to keep the chicken warm. Add the red onion and most of the remaining herbs (reserving some for garnish) to the cooking liquor and simmer until the liquid is reduced to a sauce. Add lemon juice to taste. Discard the cinnamon.

Cut up the chicken, removing the fat, and pile the pieces on a warm, deep serving plate. Pour the chunky sauce over the chicken and sprinkle it with the remaining parsley and cilantro.

Yield: 4 servings

Heat Scale: Mild

A Suspect Remedy

"To 'cool' the mouth after indulging in too much pepper, you might try the old Sherbro trick: Pull a burning stick from the fireplace and pass it back and forth an inch or so from your open mouth. It is supposed to draw off the heat."

Ellen Gibson Wilson

MOROCCAN PIGEON PIE (B'STILLA)

Known as one of the great dishes of North Africa, this first course is eaten in a specific manner: The thumb and first two fingers of the right hand are plunged through the crust into the steaming filling and the desired morsel is pulled out. In Morocco, the crust is made of tissue-thin *warka,* but if you are not in Morocco, phyllo pastry works very well.

2	young pigeons, or 1 medium chicken, cut apart at all the joints	5	tablespoons vegetable oil Salt and pepper
2	red onions, grated	2	bunches cilantro, chopped
½	teaspoon ground ginger	2	bunches parsley, chopped
1	teaspoon cayenne	8	small eggs, beaten
½	teaspoon crushed saffron threads	10	sheets phyllo pastry
2½	teaspoons ground cinnamon, plus additional for decoration	¾	cup coarsely chopped, blanched almonds, toasted Powdered sugar (optional)

Put the poultry in a large saucepan with the onions, ginger, cayenne, saffron, ½ teaspoon of the cinnamon, 3 tablespoons of the oil, and salt and pepper to taste. Add just a little water so that the birds will be pot-roasted and not boiled. Cover and cook gently, turning the poultry occasionally until tender.

Remove the pieces from the pan and set aside until cool enough to handle. Discard the skin and bones.

Add the cilantro and parsley to the pan and boil until reduced to a thick, dryish sauce. Over a very low heat, stir in the eggs to scramble them. Remove from the heat.

Preheat the oven to 375 degrees. Thoroughly oil a metal baking tin about 13 inches in diameter and 2 inches deep. Lay a sheet of phyllo pastry in the tin, fitting it to the shape of the tin and allowing any loose edges to fall over the sides. Brush with oil. Repeat with four more sheets, brushing with oil, so that the tin is completely covered.

Cover the pastry with the pigeon or chicken pieces, then the egg mixture. Cover with a small sheet of pastry and scatter the almonds over the top. Sprinkle with the remaining 2 teaspoons of cinnamon and a little powdered sugar if you like. Fold the overhanging edges of the pastry over the almonds, then cover with the remaining pastry, brushing each sheet with oil. Tuck the edges inside the tin and under the pie.

Bake for about 45 minutes until crisp and golden. Sieve powdered sugar over the top and make a lattice with ground cinnamon. Serve hot.

Yield: 8 servings

Heat Scale: Mild

African Words We Use Every Day

- "Gombo" is the West African word for okra.
- "Yam" derives from the west African verb *nyami,* which means "to eat."
- "Banana" came to America from Africa, by way of Portuguese explorers, with its spelling intact.

CHICKEN TIKKA

This recipe is an East African variation on a favorite dish served in Indian restaurants.

1½ tablespoons crushed fresh ginger

1½ tablespoons crushed fresh garlic

4 green chiles, such as jalapeños, seeds and stems removed, chopped

2 tablespoons chopped fresh cilantro

Juice of two large lemons

1 tablespoon plus 1 teaspoon vinegar

1 teaspoon salt

A pinch of ground red cayenne pepper

¼ teaspoon ground turmeric

1 teaspoon curry powder

3 tablespoons plain yogurt

4 tablespoons vegetable oil

1 chicken (3 pounds), quartered, skin scored to absorb the spices

Grind together the ginger, garlic, chiles, and cilantro with a mortar and pestle. Add the lemon juice, vinegar, all the other spices, yogurt, and 3 tablespoons of the oil. Toss with the chicken pieces and marinate at room temperature for 3 hours.

Place the chicken on the barbecue over hot coals, turning often and brushing with the remaining oil until the chicken is well browned and cooked through.

Serve with a rice dish from Chapter 8.

Yield: 4 servings

Heat Scale: Medium

CHICKEN WITH SPINACH AND YOGURT

This dish is a modern variation of an ancient West African dish that used many kinds of greens. We've substituted spinach, as it is easily accessible and works well in conjunction with the many herbs and spices in this recipe.

1 cup plain yogurt	3 green chiles, such as jalapeños, seeds and stems removed, chopped
2 cups finely chopped spinach	
1 cup finely chopped fresh cilantro	1 teaspoon crushed fresh garlic
½ cup finely chopped fresh mint	1 teaspoon crushed fresh ginger
1 chicken (2 pounds), cut into pieces	1 teaspoon ground coriander
½ cup vegetable oil	1 teaspoon ground cumin
1 medium onion, grated	1 teaspoon ground turmeric
2 medium tomatoes, finely chopped	1 teaspoon salt

Combine the yogurt, spinach, cilantro, and mint. Coat the chicken well with the mixture and allow to marinate for 1 hour.

Heat the oil and brown the onion in the oil. Add the tomatoes, chiles, garlic, ginger, all the spices, and the salt. Then add the chicken, along with its green marinade. Cook slowly and simmer, stirring frequently, until you can see oil and the chicken is tender.

Serve with the Tanzania Pineapple and Nut Salad (see recipe, p. 234).

Yield: 4 to 6 servings

Heat Scale: Hot

EAST AFRICAN SPICED AND ROASTED CHICKEN

Cayenne, red chile, and coconut milk offer an interesting twist to a usual dish. Feel free to use lite coconut milk if you are concerned about the fat or calorie count; with all of the wonderful spices in the sauce, you won't miss the extra richness a bit!

1 chicken (4½ pounds)
2 tablespoons softened butter, plus extra for basting
3 cloves garlic, crushed
1 teaspoon freshly ground black pepper
1 teaspoon ground turmeric
1 teaspoon cayenne
½ teaspoon ground cumin
1 teaspoon dried thyme
1 tablespoon finely chopped fresh cilantro
¼ cup thick coconut milk
¼ cup medium-dry sherry
1 teaspoon tomato paste
  Salt
2 teaspoons red chile powder

Remove the giblets from the chicken, if necessary, rinse out the cavity, and pat the skin dry.

Put the butter and all the remaining ingredients in a bowl and mix together to form a thick paste.

Gently ease the skin of the chicken away from the flesh and rub generously with the herb-and-butter mixture. Rub more of the mixture over the skin, legs, and wings of the chicken and into the neck cavity.

Place the chicken in a roasting pan, cover loosely with foil, and marinate overnight in the refrigerator.

Preheat the oven to 375 degrees. Cover the chicken with clean foil and roast for 1 hour, then turn the chicken over and baste with the pan juices. Cover again with foil and cook for 30 minutes.

Remove the foil and place the chicken breast-side up. Rub with a little extra butter and roast for a further 10 to 15 minutes or until the meat juices run clear and the skin is golden brown.

Serve with a rice dish or a salad.

Yield: 6 servings

Heat Scale: Medium

Unusual African Poultry

"Among the birds, flamingo was considered the greatest delicacy of all. Again, when I came on the scene, the flamingo, happily, was protected. I have never tasted it, but nonetheless it is still brought surreptitiously to some esoteric tables in remote regions. The indefatigable Leipoldt cannot praise the flamingo too highly, but strangely he makes little of the bustard, or wild peacock, as the old pioneers called it. When I tasted it I thought it better than any Christmas turkey."

Laurens van der Post

YASSA AU POULET

This truly hot West African dish features the habanero chiles, and guarantees a burst of flavor. We suggest that you serve this with slices of melon to enhance the citrus flavors and to offer a cool, sweet respite for your palate.

2	cups sliced onion	1	tablespoon salt
3	cloves garlic, minced	1	cup lemon juice
½	teaspoon minced fresh habanero chile	1¼	cups water
½	teaspoon ground ginger	5	tablespoons peanut oil
1	teaspoon white pepper	1	chicken (3 pounds), quartered
		1	green melon, cut into wedges

In a large baking dish, combine the onion, garlic, chile, ginger, pepper, and salt. Stir in the lemon juice, 1 cup of the water, and 1 tablespoon of the oil. Coat the chicken pieces in the marinade, and refrigerate for at least 4 hours, turning the pieces every 30 minutes.

Remove the chicken from the marinade, reserving the marinade, and pat the pieces dry with paper towels. In a skillet, heat the remaining 4 tablespoons of oil until it is hot but not smoking. Brown the chicken in the oil a few pieces at a time, turning frequently to brown evenly. Pour off all but about 2 tablespoons of oil from the skillet and remove it from the heat.

Using the back of a spoon, press the marinade through a fine sieve set over a bowl. Reheat the oil in the skillet and add the solids from the sieve. Cook, stirring constantly, until the onion is transparent, about 5 minutes.

Return the chicken to the skillet and add ½ cup of the strained marinade liquid and the remaining ¼ cup of the water. Bring to a boil over high heat. Partly cover the pan, reduce the heat, and simmer for about 25 minutes or until the chicken is tender.

Serve with a wedge of melon on each plate.

Yield: 4 servings

Heat Scale: Hot

ZANZIBAR DUCK

From Zanzibar, this East African recipe features ancient spices such as cloves, the most important spice and scent of Zanzibar. This dish is said to have been a favorite for the sultans of Persia.

1   duck (5 pounds)
¼   cup vegetable oil
2   cups chicken broth
12   whole cloves
2   fresh red chiles, such as cayenne or jalapeño, seeds and stems removed, chopped

½   cup orange juice
2   tablespoons lime juice
½   cup chopped red bell pepper
¼   teaspoon salt
    Orange wedges studded with cloves for garnish

Preheat the oven to 350 degrees. Pat the duck dry and remove fat from the cavity. Poke the duck around the thighs, lower breast, and back with a sharp knife.

In a large Dutch oven or roaster, heat the oil over moderate heat. Brown the duck in the oil on all sides for about 15 minutes. Place the duck on a platter and discard the fat.

Add 1 cup of the chicken broth to Dutch oven and bring it to a boil. Stir in the cloves and chiles, and turn off the heat.

Place the duck in the liquid, cover the pan, and bake for 1 hour.

After it is done, remove the duck from the oven and place it on a platter. Skim off as much fat as possible and discard. Also discard the chiles and cloves.

Next add the remaining 1 cup of chicken broth to what is left and stir and scrape the brown bits into the liquid. Bring the liquid to a boil. Add the orange juice, lime juice, bell pepper, and salt to the mixture. Return the duck to the pan and baste with the sauce. Cover and bake for 20 more minutes. Baste again.

Serve with the sauce and a steaming bowl of rice. Garnish with orange wedges.

Yield: 4 servings

Heat Scale: Medium to Hot

161

Spiced and Curried Seafood

In this chapter, you'll discover Africa's interesting selections of both fresh and saltwater fish. Powerful and primitive, strong and subtle, the seafoods of Africa are some of the finest in the world.

Piri-piri means "peppers" in Swahili, and it is the spice of honor in our first two recipes, Crab Claws *Piri-Piri* (p. 166) and Shrimp *Piri-Piri* (p. 167). We follow with another Swahili recipe collected by our friend Michelle Cox, Baked Fish, Swahili Style (p. 168). The spicy sauce that accompanies this recipe is so good you'll want to keep some extra on hand.

You might pucker up a bit when tasting the next Ethiopian dish, Curried Prawns in Pineapple (p. 169). We think you'll find the sweet yet tart flavors of this recipe addictive. And, based on the title alone, who could resist our next selection, Pastry with the Devil Inside (p. 170)? For a real thrill, we suggest you substitute a red habanero for the jalapeños in the recipe. The Red Chile–Stewed Sea Bass (p. 172) from Mozambique also offers a fiery flavor, with New Mexico red chiles heating things up a bit.

Our next recipe is our most exotic: Crocodile Chile Curry (p. 174) from Kenya. Feel free to substitute alligator meat or another firm fish if you can't locate any croc at your favorite grocery store. This is one critter that definitely doesn't taste like chicken!

Also from Kenya, our next entrée is Green Masala Fish (p. 175). We enjoy this served with a side of steaming *basmati* rice (available at any supermarket). Rice is also a part of our next recipe, Tanzanian Fiery Fried Fish and Rice (p. 176). One can often find this sold at stands in the markets of East Africa, along with a side of hot sauce.

North Africa is known for its production of excellent almonds. Many recipes from this region, such as Almond-Coated Baked Fish (p. 177) and Apple-and-Almond Hake with Spicy Parsley Sauce (p. 178), feature this rich nut.

A spiced-out oil is the star of our next selection, Marinated Fish Cooked in Spiced Oil (p. 180). And if you are really trying to impress a loved one, fix the Curried Lobster with Rice (p. 181). This jewel of the sea is not only extremely rare in West Africa, but very expensive as well.

East and South Africa are the origins of our next two recipes, Hellish Hake (p. 182) and Paprika-Grilled Fish (p. 183). Both are great choices if you are counting calories and watching your bottom line.

Our last three entrées are all excellent choices. Just add your favorite dry white wine to the Tunisian Broiled Shrimp (p. 184), Seafood Strudel with Sweet and Hot Pepper Sauce (p. 186), or Monkfish Curry with Fresh Fruit (p. 185), and you've got a feast fit for the sultans.

CRAB CLAWS PIRI-PIRI

Our friend, Michelle Cox, collected this recipe from the Driftwood Beach Club in Malindi, Kenya. According to Michelle, there's only one variety of chile powder (ground chile) available there, of medium to low heat. She suggests that you choose any variety you like; New Mexico red chile is a perfect pick.

2	pounds crab claws, cooked	2	tablespoons tomato paste
4	tablespoons butter	4	ounces white wine
2	teaspoons garlic, minced		Juice of one lime
2	tablespoons red chile powder, such as New Mexican	2	tablespoons parsley or cilantro, chopped fine

Partly crack the crab claws so that the sauce will be able to soak in. Melt the butter in a deep-sided frying pan over low heat. Add all of the remaining ingredients except the parsley. Cook slowly until the wine is cooked off and the flavors blend, about 15 minutes.

Add the crab claws and increase the heat. Carefully toss the claws in the sauce until warmed through.

Sprinkle with parsley and serve with rice and lime wedges.

Yield: 2 servings

Heat Scale: Medium

SHRIMP PIRI-PIRI

Shellfish is abundant off the African coast, and the prawns are so large that a couple of them will make a meal. The Mozambique marinade not only goes well with shrimp or prawns, but also with fish and chicken.

Please note: this recipe requires advance preparation.

Marinade

¼ cup butter or margarine

¼ cup peanut oil

2 tablespoons crushed dried *piri-piri* chile (or substitute *piquins*), seeds included

4 cloves garlic, minced

3 tablespoons lime or lemon juice, preferably fresh

1 pound raw, large prawns, shelled and deveined

Melt the butter and add the oil and the remaining marinade ingredients. Simmer for a couple of minutes to blend the flavors.

Toss the shrimp in the marinade and marinate for 2 hours.

Thread the shrimp on skewers and grill over charcoal, or broil, basting with the marinade, until done.

Heat the marinade and serve it on the side.

Yield: 4 servings

Heat Scale: Medium

BAKED FISH, SWAHILI STYLE

Swahili cooking involves heavy use of local ingredients, such as coconut milk, tomatoes, and chiles. Michelle Cox collected this recipe from Kenya. Michelle says that tamarind pulp would normally be used as a tangy ingredient to cut the heaviness of coconut milk, but lime is an adequate substitute and is commonly used. As a variation, make the sauce ahead and serve with a grilled, whole fish.

2	tablespoons ghee or cooking oil	2¼	cups coconut milk
3	small green peppers, chopped	2¼	cups fish stock
3	medium tomatoes, chopped	1	tablespoon turmeric powder or mild curry powder
1	small onion, chopped		Salt and pepper
3	Kenya chiles (or substitute red jalapeño), seeds and stems removed, chopped fine	3	fish fillets (7 ounces each) Juice of three limes
2	tablespoons cornstarch		

Preheat the oven to 350 degrees. Heat a couple of tablespoons of the ghee or cooking oil in an ovenproof frying pan over medium heat. Sauté the green peppers, tomatoes, onions, and chiles until they are just cooked, then lower the heat.

Next add the cornstarch, coconut milk, fish stock, and turmeric. Cook slowly until thickened. Season to taste with salt and pepper.

Place the fish fillets in a large frying pan, cover with the sauce, and sprinkle with the lime juice. Bake in the oven for 15 to 20 minutes until the fish is cooked.

Serve with your favorite rice from Chapter 8.

Yield: 3 servings

Heat Scale: Medium

CURRIED PRAWNS IN PINEAPPLE

This Ethiopian dish offers a very unusual and beautiful presentation, as well as a taste of India through the use of curry. While Red Sea prawns are called for, any large shrimp or prawns from your local fish market will work.

1½	pounds fresh prawns	2	teaspoons curry powder
	Juice of one lemon	½	teaspoon cayenne
2	tablespoons oil	½	pint stock, from fish or prawns
1	onion, chopped	1	ounce margarine
1	tablespoon chopped chives or green onions, plus additional for garnish	¼	cup flour
2	tomatoes, chopped	1	large or 2 small pineapples (for individual dishes, use small pineapples)

Boil the prawns for 10 minutes in salted water. Peel off the shells and remove the black vein running down the back. Sprinkle with lemon juice.

Heat the oil in a large frying pan, and fry the onion, chives, and tomato with the curry powder and cayenne. Cook for 5 minutes, then add the stock and prawns and simmer over low heat for 15 minutes.

Mix the margarine and flour together and add a little at a time to the prawns, stirring until smooth. Cook a little longer.

Halve the pineapples lengthwise and cut out some of the flesh. Fill the hollows with the prawn mixture and sprinkle with more chopped chives.

Yield: 4 servings

Heat Scale: Mild

PASTRY WITH THE DEVIL INSIDE (PASTEL COM DIABO DENTRO)

This recipe originates in the Cape Verde Islands, a former Portuguese colony located just off the western tip of Africa. It is an unusual dish, and should be prepared with tuna that is as fresh as possible. For corn flour, check natural foods groceries, or make your own by grinding corn meal in a food processor until it is extremely fine.

2 large sweet potatoes, unpeeled	2 red jalapeño chiles, seeds and stems removed, finely chopped, or 1 teaspoon cayenne
1 to 2 cups corn flour	
1 medium onion, finely chopped	
2 tablespoons olive oil	1 teaspoon salt
1 pound fresh tuna, cooked	Oil for deep-frying
1 medium tomato, chopped	

To make the pastry, wash the potatoes well and boil them until they are very tender. Place them in a food processor and blend until they make a smooth paste, or mash them thoroughly in a large bowl, making sure to get out all the lumps. Slowly add the corn flour, blending it in with your hands or with a wooden spoon to make a stiff dough. The moisture in the potatoes will determine how much corn flour you need, but the mixture should resemble biscuit dough or a course pie pastry. If the dough becomes too dry, add a few spoonfuls of the water in which the potatoes were cooked. Roll into a ball, wrap in a damp, lint-free cloth, and chill while you make the filling.

Sauté the onion in the oil until it becomes translucent. Flake the tuna and mix with the onions, tomatoes, chiles or cayenne, and salt.

Unwrap the dough and spread the damp towel on a flat surface. Working on top of the towel, tear off golf-ball size pieces of the dough and roll them into circles about ⅛ inch thick and 4 to 5 inches in diameter. Put a tablespoonful of the tuna filling on half of the dough circle; fold the other half of the circle across it and pinch the edges to seal.

In a deep, heavy pot, heat oil for frying until a test piece of dough sputters vigorously. You may either deep-fry the turnovers or fry them in a couple of inches of oil, turning them once to allow both sides to cook. The oil is the right temperature when a test turnover becomes golden brown after frying about 3 minutes on each side. Fry 2 or 3 pastries at a time, continuing to make more as you fry the first ones. Drain on clean, absorbent cloths, and serve immediately.

Yield: 14–16 pastries

Heat Scale: Medium

Ancient African Seafood

"The drying and smoking of meat and fish, practiced all over our planet, goes back to the time when men first learned to use fire. Salting implies the proximity of a source of salt, either sea salt or mineral salt, or of trading posts along the salt routes. Fish preserved by drying, smoking, or salting still constitutes a large part of the African diet, and some of the techniques employed have not changed for thousands of years."

Maguelonne Toussaint-Samat

RED CHILE-STEWED SEA BASS (MOZAMBICAN PEITE LUMBO)

Mozambicans have been known to throw whole handfuls of chile into dishes all at once. We certainly like their thinking, and find this particularly spicy, zesty dish to be most delightful.

1	sea bass, grouper, or baby cod fish (3 pounds)	3	tablespoons dried New Mexican red chile powder
2	cups lemon juice	2	red onions, chopped finely
2	cups water	½	teaspoon ground nutmeg
	Salt and pepper to taste	¾	tablespoon ground dried shrimp
3	tablespoons palm or peanut oil	½	cup coconut milk
2	bell peppers, deribbed and chopped finely	½	cup grated coconut
2	medium-sized tomatoes, skinned and sieved	¼	teaspoon ground coriander
		1	pound shrimp, shelled and deveined, with shells reserved

Clean, eviscerate, and wash the fish, leaving the head on and the eyes out. Mix the lemon juice with the water, and acidulate the fish in the lemon water for a few minutes. Next, season the fish with salt and pepper inside and out, and refrigerate until ready to cook.

Heat the palm oil in a skillet and sauté the bell peppers, tomatoes, chile powder, onions, nutmeg, and ground dried shrimp for 7 minutes. Add the coconut milk, grated coconut, and coriander, and simmer covered for 15 minutes, stirring periodically.

Place the marinated fish and the whole shrimp in a pan large enough to hold the fish intact, and pour the sauce over them. Add a little water at this point if necessary. Cover with foil and simmer for 15 minutes. Stir only once, without breaking the fish, then simmer covered for another 10 minutes or so. Add water only as needed, and in small amounts.

Serve with Mashed Pungent Pumpkin (see recipe, p. 207).

Yield: 4 to 6 servings

Heat Scale: Medium

And These Snails Measure Six Inches in Length!

"The Ashanti people and others of West Africa actually value giant African snails equally with goat, mutton, and beef in preference to pork, chicken, or fish. They usually kill the snail by heating it in water and then remove it from the shell, wash the fresh soft parts, and use them immediately in local dishes. They also skewer a number on a stick and smoke them over a wood fire until they are well dried. Snails provide about half of the daily animal protein consumed by many West African peoples."

Calvin W. Schwabe

CROCODILE CHILE CURRY

This is surely the most exotic African curry we came across. This recipe is from Michelle Cox in Malindi, Kenya, who says she is lucky enough to have a crocodile farm nearby. "But if you're short on croc tail, the recipe is great for octopus," she says. Alligator or another firm fish can also be substituted.

1¼ pounds crocodile meat, boned, or 1½ pounds octopus	1 heaping tablespoon fresh crushed ginger
½ cup vegetable oil	2½ tablespoons ground coriander
3 large onions, peeled and sliced	1½ tablespoons cumin powder
3 large ripe tomatoes, or 1 can tomatoes, peeled and sliced	2 tablespoons curry powder
2 habanero chiles, seeded and chopped	3 cubes beef stock
1 heaping tablespoon crushed garlic	1 tablespoon sugar
	1 tablespoon lime juice
	Salt
	3 tablespoons chopped cilantro

Cube the crocodile into 1-inch pieces. If using octopus, remove the beak and eyes and cut into ½-inch pieces.

Heat the oil in a heavy saucepan and sauté the onions and tomatoes until soft. Add the chiles, garlic, and ginger, and cook over low heat, stirring. After about 30 seconds, add the spice powders and stir, taking care not to burn.

Add the crocodile or octopus, with sufficient water to cover, plus the beef stock cubes, sugar, and lime juice. Boil gently for at least 30 minutes. Stir occasionally to avoid sticking. Add water when necessary.

When the meat is tender, season with salt and add the cilantro.

Serve with rice.

Yield: 4 servings
Heat Scale: Hot

GREEN MASALA FISH

This East African recipe by way of India is one that can be enjoyed by all, as it can be adapted to many tastes. First, prawns may be substituted for the fish fillets. Second, New Mexican chile can be used as part of the chile requirement if less heat is desired. And third, you can use onion or garlic, depending on your tastes.

2	pounds fish fillets	1	tablespoon salt
2	tablespoons fresh cilantro	1	tablespoon chopped garlic, or onion
2	tablespoons fresh mint or basil		
6	Kenya chiles, or red jalapeños, seeds and stems removed, chopped	2	tablespoons chopped fresh ginger
5	tablespoons ground cumin	2	tablespoons oil
5	tablespoons grated coconut	½	cup lime juice

Place the fish in a shallow dish to marinate. Put the cilantro, mint, and chiles in a blender or food processor. Add the cumin, coconut, salt, garlic, and ginger. Blend to a fine paste. Mix in one tablespoon each of the oil and lime juice. Coat the fish with the spice mixture and leave to marinate for 30 minutes.

Preheat the broiler pan on high heat. Brush the remaining oil on the pan to prevent sticking. Put the fish under the broiler for 2 minutes, then reduce the heat or lower the pan and grill the fish, basting with the remaining lime juice, until the fish is cooked but not dry.

Yield: 4 servings

Heat Scale: Hot

TANZANIAN FIERY FRIED FISH AND RICE (WALI NA SAMAKI)

Tanzania, formerly called Tanganyika, is on the east coast of Africa. It is home to Mount Kilimanjaro, as well as many tropical beaches and great lakes, which provide an abundance of interesting fish perfect for fiery recipes such as this.

4	large tomatoes, sliced	½	cup vegetable oil, plus additional for frying
2	bell peppers, sliced in rings	2	bay leaves
2	jalapeño chiles, seeds and stems removed, chopped	2	cups water
2	onions, chopped	4	pounds red snapper or halibut
	Juice and peel of one lemon	1	cup flour
1	tablespoon salt	4	cups cooked rice
1	tablespoon pepper		

Cook the tomatoes, bell pepper, jalapeños, onions, lemon juice and peel, salt, pepper, oil, bay leaves, and the water in a large saucepan over moderate heat for 25 minutes.

Cut the fish into 4-ounce pieces and rub with salt and pepper, then dip in the flour. Brown in ½ inch of hot oil until tender.

To serve, place the cooked rice on a large platter. Put the fish on top of rice and pour the sauce over everything.

Yield: 8 servings

Heat Scale: Medium

ALMOND-COATED BAKED FISH (HUT BENOUA)

This unusual sweet entrée is made both beautiful and hot by startling red paprika. With origins in the Moroccan fishing port of Safi, this is quite a delicious fish dish with its crisp, sweet, spiced coating.

1½ cups blanched almonds, toasted and ground

½ cup plus 1 tablespoon powdered sugar

1 tablespoon orange-flower water

1 tablespoon ground cinnamon

2 teaspoons hot paprika

½ cup water

¼ cup butter, softened, plus extra for buttering
Salt and pepper

1 sea bass (4 pounds), cleaned

1 onion, finely chopped
A pinch of saffron threads, crushed

Preheat the oven to 375 degrees. Put the almonds, powdered sugar, orange-flower water, cinnamon, paprika, 3 tablespoons of the water, half the butter, and salt and pepper to taste in a bowl, and mix to a smooth paste. Season the fish inside and out, then fill it with half the almond mixture.

Mix the onion, saffron, and remaining water together, and pour into a large buttered baking dish. Put the fish on the onion mixture and spread the remaining almond mixture over the fish. Melt the remaining butter and trickle it over the almond mixture.

Bake for about 45 minutes, until the fish is cooked and the almond topping has a crust on it yet is still soft underneath.

Yield: 4 servings

Heat Scale: Medium

Apple-and-Almond Hake with Spicy Parsley Sauce

A dusting of cayenne enhances this South African recipe, and the apples, lemons, and almonds create a textural delight. Feel free to substitute any firm white fish for the hake.

4	large hake or other fish fillets (6–8 ounces each)		2	ounces butter, plus extra if needed
	Salt and freshly ground black pepper		1	tablespoon sunflower oil
¼	cup flour		2	tablespoons cake flour
3	teaspoons cayenne		2	tablespoons chopped parsley
2	Granny Smith apples		1	jalapeño chile, seeds and stems removed, minced
	Juice from one lemon		¼	cup dry white wine
2	ounces slivered almonds		½	cup cream
			2	teaspoons fresh lemon juice

Season the hake with salt and pepper and dust lightly with the flour and cayenne. Slice the apples into wedges and sprinkle with lemon juice to prevent discoloring.

Heat a nonstick frying pan and toast the almonds over gentle heat, tossing them to brown evenly, then set the almonds aside.

Add the butter and oil to the frying pan and lightly brown the apple wedges very quickly so that they do not become mushy. Set the apples aside separately from the almonds.

Increase the heat and fry the fish, adding butter if necessary. The cooking time will be about 4 to 5 minutes, at which point the fish should be crispy-brown and perfectly cooked. Transfer the fish to a warmed serving platter and keep it warm while preparing the sauce.

With the pan off the heat, blend the flour, parsley, and jalapeño into the pan juices. Slowly add the wine, cream, and lemon juice, then stir over high heat for a couple of minutes until the sauce is smooth and thickened. Add a little water if the sauce is too thick, and season with salt and pepper. Pour the sauce into a separate serving bowl.

To retain the crispness of the fish, garnish the platter with apple wedges, scatter over the toasted almonds, and serve the sauce separately.

Yield: 4 servings

Heat Scale: Medium

Not Your Usual Perch

Anglers on the Nile and its tributaries get excited when they hook into the Nile perch, for it can weigh up to 300 pounds. Unfortunately, the flesh of these fish, if they weigh more than twenty pounds, is often coarse. The Nile perch was so revered by the ancient Egyptians that they mummified it. Interestingly, neither the priests nor the Pharaohs were permitted to eat it.

MARINATED FISH COOKED IN SPICED OIL (POISSON EN TAJINE MQUALLI)

This Tunisian dish is a classic. Feel free to switch the fish to one of your liking; halibut can be replaced by hake, cod, or gray mullet in this recipe.

3   cloves garlic
    A pinch of salt
1   teaspoon cayenne pepper
1   teaspoon ground coriander
1   teaspoon cumin
2   pounds halibut steaks

¾   cup olive oil
1   teaspoon ground ginger
    A pinch of saffron threads, crushed
    Stoned black olives for garnish
    Lemon quarters for garnish

To make the marinade, crush the garlic with a large pinch of salt, then mix with the cayenne, coriander, and cumin.

Rub each halibut with the marinade, then put in a single layer in a heavy baking dish and leave in a cool place for 6 hours.

Preheat the oven to 375 degrees.

Mix the oil with the ginger and saffron. Pour over the fish, cover, and bake for about 20 to 25 minutes, until the fish flakes easily.

Serve garnished with olives and lemons, with your favorite salad from Chapter 3.

Yield: 4 to 6 servings

Heat Scale: Mild

CURRIED LOBSTER WITH RICE

This West African recipe features lobsters, which are scarce and difficult to catch, making them a special and expensive meal. Crab meat is often substituted, as it is much more affordable and accessible.

2	live lobsters (2 pounds each)	1	cup tomato sauce
1	cup fresh shrimp	½	teaspoon nutmeg
2	cups chopped onion	2	tablespoons Malawi Curry
2	tablespoons lemon juice		Powder (see recipe, p. 14)
⅔	cup melted butter	1	teaspoon powdered ginger
1	cup cubed eggplant	2	teaspoons cayenne
	or cucumber	2	cups coconut milk (optional)
	Salt and garlic powder to taste	4	cups cooked rice

Wash the lobster and shrimp, and boil for 7 to 10 minutes in salted water with 1 tablespoon of the chopped onions. When cooked, remove the lobster meat from the shell and cut into pieces. Reserve the stock and shells.

Peel the shrimp, devein and wash, then sprinkle both lobster meat and shrimp with lemon juice.

Heat the butter in a large skillet and sauté the remaining onion for 5 minutes. Add the eggplant or cucumber, lobster meat, shrimp, salt, and garlic powder. Cook for another 10 minutes.

Pour the tomato sauce over the entire mixture, then stir in the remaining spices, one after the other. Add the reserved stock or coconut milk. Simmer, stirring from time to time, for 20 minutes.

Serve the dish hot. For a festive touch, fill the lobster or crab shells halfway with hot boiled rice and spoon the sauce over the rice.

Yield: 4 to 6 servings

Heat Scale: Medium

HELLISH HAKE

You'll think you've arrived in heaven when you taste this habanero hot fish dish. Direct from the coast of East Africa, this recipe is wonderful with a generous helping of ginger and habanero.

4	hake fillets, skinned and trimmed	1	habanero chile, stem and seeds removed, minced
	Salt and white pepper	2	eggs, lightly beaten
	Juice of one lemon	4	bananas
¼	cup toasted bread crumbs		Butter and sunflower oil for frying
¼	cup flaked coconut		
2	teaspoons grated ginger		

Season the hake with salt and pepper and a squeeze of lemon juice. Mix together the bread crumbs, coconut, ginger, and chile. Dip the fillets in the egg, then in the crumb mixture, pressing the fish firmly into the mixture.

Peel the bananas, cut them in half lengthwise, and sprinkle them with lemon juice. Fry the bananas gently in sizzling butter until light golden-brown. Take care not to overcook them, or they'll get mushy. Remove from the pan and set aside.

Heat more butter in the same frying pan, add a dash of oil, and fry the fish until golden-brown and cooked through to the bone. Drain the fish briefly on paper towels, place on hot serving plates, and top each one with a fried banana.

Yield: 4 servings

Heat Scale: Medium

PAPRIKA-GRILLED FISH

Paprika adds the extra zing to this South African recipe. Many South African fish have unusual names, such as *geelbek, kob, kingklip,* and *steenbras.* We suggest using yellowtail snapper for a superb meal. Note: The sauce may be made a couple of days ahead and reheated.

4	large fish steaks (6–8 ounces each) Salt and freshly ground black pepper to taste	1	tablespoon chopped basil leaves
3½	tablespoons butter	2	teaspoons hot paprika Squeeze of fresh lemon juice
2	tablespoons chopped parsley	⅔	cup cream

Heat the broiler. Arrange the fish on an oiled grilling tray and season with salt and pepper.

Melt the butter in a small saucepan and mix in the parsley, basil, paprika, and the squeeze of lemon juice. Brush half of this mixture over the fish and grill for 3 to 4 minutes. Turn the fish, brush with the remaining buttery mixture, and grill for another 2 to 4 minutes until cooked. Transfer the fish to a heated serving platter.

Pour the cream into the grilling pan and cook on the stovetop, stirring in all the buttery fish juices. Pour the sauce over the fish and garnish with an extra sprinkling of paprika.

Serve with a green salad and your favorite side dish from Chapter 8.

Yield: 4 servings

Heat Scale: Medium

TUNISIAN BROILED SHRIMP

There's something succulent about broiled shrimp that makes your mouth water just thinking about them. This Tunisian specialty is no different: cloves, cumin, ginger, and cayenne combine for a fragrant, feisty delight.

4	pounds raw shrimp in the shell	1	teaspoon paprika
2	cloves garlic, crushed	1	teaspoon cayenne pepper
¼	cup olive oil	1	bunch cilantro, finely chopped
1	teaspoon ground cumin		Salt
½	teaspoon ground ginger		Lemon and lime wedges

Remove the heads and legs from the shrimp. Using kitchen scissors, cut the shrimp in half lengthwise, leaving the tails intact. Lay the shrimp in a single layer in a large, shallow dish.

In a small bowl, mix together the remaining ingredients, minus the lemon and lime wedges. Pour the spice mixture over the shrimp and leave in a cool place for 1 to 2 hours, turning the shrimp occasionally.

Preheat the broiler. Broil the shrimp for 3 to 4 minutes, until they turn pink, brushing with any remaining marinade as they cook.

Serve with lemon and lime wedges.

Yield: 4 servings
Heat Scale: Medium

MONKFISH CURRY WITH FRESH FRUIT

Here's another tasty, unusual South African seafood dish, featuring—of course—the ever-popular curries.

½ cup dry white wine
1 cup fish stock
1 cup cream
1 small onion, finely diced
4 cloves fresh ginger, finely crushed
2 teaspoons Malawi Curry Powder (see recipe, p. 14)

10 tablespoons cold butter
2 pounds monkfish filets cut into large dice
Flour for dredging
Squeeze of fresh lemon juice
Salt and white pepper to taste
Fresh sliced fruit in season for garnish

To make the sauce, place the white wine and fish stock in a saucepan over high heat and reduce by two-thirds. Add the cream and simmer for 5 minutes.

In a frying pan, sauté the onion, ginger, and curry powder in 6 tablespoons of the butter, to allow the curry to release its flavor.

Dredge the monkfish in the flour, add it to the curry, and cook through.

Just before serving, whisk the remaining cold butter into the sauce to thicken it. Finally, add a squeeze of lemon, salt, and pepper to sharpen the flavor. Pour the sauce into the pan with the monkfish and combine gently.

Serve with saffron rice and garnish with slices of whatever fresh fruit is available.

Yield: 4 to 6 servings

Heat Scale: Mild

SEAFOOD STRUDEL WITH SWEET AND HOT PEPPER SAUCE

This unique South African recipe features both sweet and hot red peppers. We love this dish when it's prepared with fresh mussels; green lip from New Zealand are preferred.

2	pounds diced seafood, shrimp, mussels, and whitefish
½	cup butter
1¼	cups white wine
2½	cups cream
	Small bunch of fresh dill or chervil, chopped
1	package commercial phyllo pastry

The Sauce

4	tablespoons butter
3½	large red bell peppers, seeds and stems removed, diced (the ½ pepper is julienned for garnish)
2	red jalapeño chiles, seeds and stems removed, minced
½	onion, diced
2	cups cream
	Paprika
	Salt and white pepper

In a large pan, sauté the diced seafood in ¼ cup of the butter until just firm. Remove the seafood from the pan and allow it to cool.

Add the white wine to the pan and reduce it by two-thirds. Add the cream and reduce again to a coating consistency. Add the chopped dill or chervil. Mix the seafood into the sauce and allow it to cool, but not to get cold.

Preheat the oven to 375 degrees.

Melt the remaining ¼ cup of butter. Working quickly with the phyllo pastry (it dries very fast), lay out a large square of about 3 to 4 thicknesses. Brush with the melted butter. Spread the seafood mixture over it and roll it up like a burrito, tucking in the ends. Brush again with melted butter, and place on a greased baking tray.

Bake for 10 to 12 minutes. Check frequently, as this is very fragile pastry.

To make the sauce, melt the butter in a saucepan and sauté the 3 diced peppers, the jalapeños, and the diced onion. Place the mixture in a blender with the cream, and process until smooth.

Return the mixture to the pan and correct the seasoning with paprika, salt, and pepper. Reduce a little, and add the remaining ½ pepper, sliced to a very fine julienne.

Carefully cut the strudel in slices and serve with the sauce and a green salad.

Yield: 4 to 6 servings

Heat Scale: Medium

What Seafood to Eat in Africa
When You Run Out of Nile Perch

- Aquarium fish called *cichlids* grow up to eighteen inches long and are commonly eaten in Africa. In North American restaurants, we know these fish as "tilapia."
- The elephant fish, which has a long snout and can reach five feet in length, is usually dried and eaten, except in East Africa, where mothers believe the flesh will cause their children to be born with similar snouts.
- The giant frog (*Rana goliath*) measures three feet from nose to toe and weighs seven pounds—and that's a lot of frog legs!
- The lungfish, which burrows into drying lakes, can live up to three years in a dried mud cocoon. It is often dug up and eaten during droughts.
- Sawfish, a type of skate, are a great delicacy in Madagascar.

Kenyan Coastal Cuisine

"At any fish market in the coastal city of Mombasa, a multitude of brightly coloured fish are laid out on wet slabs to be poked and prodded by the fussy cooks who come to buy for the next meal. For generations, the coastal people have been using fish as an important part of their diet, often preparing meals using a combination of ingredients and techniques they learned from foreign traders and explorers who visited their shores. Visitors to Kenya will never forget the lavish buffets prepared in the beach hotels, each of which tries to outdo the others in displays of marinated fish, samaki curries, and lavish shellfish arrangements."

Kathy Eldon and Eamon Mullan

Sizzling Sides and Vegetable Dishes

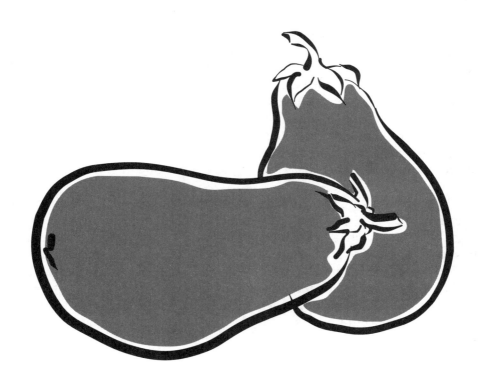

Because the majority of Africans do not have easy access to meat, fish, or poultry, vegetables and legumes have come to play a large part in the cuisine of the continent. Many vegetables are stewed and served with bread; the stewed vegetables in North Africa are called *tajines,* although *tajines* can also contain meat if it is available. There are many fertile farming areas in Africa, and it is from these areas that the people can purchase a vast variety of vegetables, as well as fruit.

It is also interesting to note that a mainstay vegetable in West Africa is okra, which the slaves brought with them to the New World. Thus we can trace the migration of okra from Africa to the American South, where "gumbo" (another term for okra) is so popular. Food is the great assimilator of cultures worldwide.

One of our first great assimilators is Swahili Beans (p. 192) from Kenya; this dish contains coconut milk and curry, indicating its Eastern influence. The dried beans, which are high in protein, are prevalent in cuisines all over the world. The next bean recipe, Sugar Bean Curry with Jalapeños (p. 193), combines the flavors of jalapeño chiles, fresh ginger, and cardamom, which spice up an otherwise bland dish. Spiced-Up Vegetarian *Jollof* Rice (p. 194) combines dried beans, fresh green beans, rice, and a variety of herbs and spices. It is a substantial side dish that should be served with a light entrée.

The Moroccan dish Aromatic Chickpea *Tajine* (p. 196) is truly aromatic, thanks to the addition of North African spices. The saffron adds a lovely light yellow color and a subtle taste. Never overuse saffron, or your dish will taste like soap! Another *tajine,* Mixed Vegetable *Tajine* (p. 198), is full of sautéed vegetables, raisins, and chile. It has a multitude of complex textures and flavors.

Two rice recipes are included here, one very simple and tasty, the other quite complex. Chile Coconut Rice (p. 199) has a unique flavor because the rice is cooked in coconut milk with a hefty dash of New Mexican green chiles. The more complex Egyptian recipe, *Koshary* (p. 200), is an unusual dish, with its six layers of ingredients and flavors. It is sold as a common street food and could be a perfect substantial meal for vegetarians.

We have also included some delicious and easy-to-make single-vegetable dishes. Spiced Glazed Carrots with Dill (p. 202) is a taste-pleaser with the addition of honey, ginger, orange juice, and dill. It is light side dish and would be good served with a rich entrée. A popular dish, Spicy West African Okra (p. 203), is highly spiced and easy to make. Serve it hot or cold as an addition to a buffet. Steamed Chile Corn (p. 204), with its green and red chiles, is a steamed side dish from Nigeria.

In Africa, yams are prepared and served just like potatoes. In Spiced and Steamed Yams (p. 205), from Nigeria, the yams are combined with spicy cayenne, and the final result has the consistency of a dumpling. Spiced Boiled Yams (p. 206) are cooked with garlic and sprinkled with incendiary *piri-piri* powder just before serving.

Pumpkin is frequently served as a vegetable side dish in Africa. Mashed Pungent Pumpkin (p. 207) is spiced up with cayenne and can be served in a casserole or formed into individual patties.

Vegetables in Peanut Sauce (p. 208), a West African side dish, is a melange of vegetables and spices, topped with a spicy peanut sauce. A North African recipe, Fried Peppers with Capers and Garlic (p. 210), contains fresh New Mexican red chiles that are fried to add a distinctive taste. It can be served hot or cold. Another North African recipe, Onion *Tajine* (p. 211), is spiced with crushed red chile. The spices and saffron add a complexity of tastes to complement the onions.

A delicious Ethiopian side dish, Fresh Tomato and Green Chile Relish (p. 212), is served chilled and goes well served with one of the more substantial entrées. Shredded, sautéed greens and chiles form the basis for Hot African Greens and Beef (p. 213); *piri-piri* sherry adds another level of flavor.

Two curry side dishes are included here. The first of these, Dried Fruit Curry (p. 214), has its origins in South Africa. A variety of dried fruits are stewed with curry powder and then garnished with bananas and chopped peanuts. It is delicious served with roasted lamb. *Frikkadel* Curry (p. 215) is another South African specialty. Spiced balls containing a small amount of meat are cooked in a rich, spicy sauce. This dish works well with any type of roasted meat.

The final set of recipes in this chapter are a variety of breads. The first recipe, *Peri-Peri* Peanut Muffins (p. 216), is very typical of African cooking, utilizing the combination of peanuts and chile. They are great to serve with any meal, and they are guaranteed to wake you up when you eat them with your morning coffee. *Injera* Bread (p. 217) does not contain any chiles, but it is the basic bread in Ethiopian cuisine, and therefore needs to be included in this chapter. The final bread recipe, *Roti* Bread (p. 218), is found in Africa wherever East Indians have made their mark on the cuisine. It can be served flat or wrapped around food, much like a tortilla.

SWAHILI BEANS (MBAAZI ZA NAZI)

This recipe was given to us by Michelle Cox of Malindi, Kenya. She says, "Beans are an inexpensive and nutritious way to get the family fed. While this is a traditional recipe, it is uncommonly popular with overseas guests at the Driftwood's Saturday night poolside barbecues." The coconut milk produces a subtle richness that completely changes the character of the beans. Any green chile can be used, and minced garlic and chopped green pepper add interest to this dish.

1	pound pigeon peas or light red kidney beans	2	green chiles, such as jalapeños, seeds and stems removed, chopped
1	cup light coconut milk	1	teaspoon salt
1	onion, sliced	1	cup thick coconut milk, or unsweetened coconut cream
1	to 2 teaspoons curry powder		

Clean, wash, and place the beans in a large pot. Add enough water to just cover the beans. Bring to a boil and continue to boil for 2 minutes. Turn off heat, cover, and allow to sit for 1 hour.

Drain the beans, place them in a large pot, cover them with cold water, and boil until they are soft and the water has been absorbed (about 1½ hours). Add more water if necessary during cooking.

Add the remaining ingredients, except for the thick coconut milk. Cook over medium heat until the mixture is almost dry.

Then add the thick coconut milk, and cook on low heat for 5 minutes.

Yield: 4 servings

Heat Scale: Mild

SUGAR BEAN CURRY WITH JALAPEÑOS

In this recipe, substitute any dry bean for the South African sugar beans. The flavors in this dish are unusual and exotic. It is a side dish that goes particularly well with lamb.

¾ pound dried South African sugar beans

2 tablespoons vegetable oil

1 cup coarsely chopped onion

3 cloves garlic, minced

3 jalapeños, seeds and stems removed, chopped

1 tablespoon chopped fresh ginger

2 sticks cinnamon (3 inches)

1 teaspoon turmeric

2 cardamom seeds

1 tablespoon Malawi Curry Powder (see recipe, p. 14)

1 cup chopped tomato

½ teaspoon salt

½ teaspoon sugar

½ cup water

Cover the beans with water and soak overnight in the refrigerator.

Drain and wash the beans, place them in a large pot, cover with water, and cook until they are soft, about 1 to 1½ hours. Drain the beans.

Heat the oil in a large, heavy skillet and sauté the onion for 3 minutes. Add the garlic and reduce the heat to a simmer. Add the chiles, ginger, cinnamon, turmeric, cardamom, curry powder, tomato, salt, sugar, and the water; cover and simmer for 20 to 30 minutes.

Add the drained beans and simmer for an additional 20 minutes.

Yield: 6 servings

Heat Scale: Medium

SPICED-UP VEGETARIAN JOLLOF RICE

This version of *Jollof* Rice from Sierra Leone differs from the previous ones because it is a vegetarian side dish. Traditionally, this recipe recommends palm oil, but we have substituted canola oil for health considerations.

1   cup dry black-eyed peas, or 1 can (16 ounces) black-eyed peas plus 1 cup vegetable stock

2   pounds eggplant, cubed

1   teaspoon salt

3   tablespoons canola oil

2   cups chopped onion

4   jalapeño chiles, seeds and stems removed, chopped

4   cloves garlic, minced

¼   cup chopped fresh ginger root

¾   cup chopped green bell pepper

4   cups chopped tomatoes

2   tablespoons tomato paste

2   tablespoons cayenne

1   teaspoon Malawi Curry Power (see recipe, p. 14)

2   teaspoons hot pepper sauce of your choice, or use one from Chapter 2

½   pound fresh green beans, cleaned and cut into 1-inch pieces

Wash the beans, cover with cold water, and soak in the refrigerator overnight.

Then drain the beans, put them in a large heavy casserole pot, cover with water, and bring them to a boil. Reduce the heat to a simmer and simmer for 1½ hours, until they are tender. If you are using canned beans, drain them and simmer in the vegetable stock.

Place the cubed eggplant in a colander, sprinkle with the salt, and let it drain for 30 minutes. Rinse off the salt, place the cubes in paper towels, and blot dry.

Heat the oil in a large ovenproof casserole pot, add the eggplant, and sauté for 2 minutes. Add the onion, chiles, garlic, ginger, bell pepper, tomatoes, tomato paste, cayenne, curry powder, and hot sauce, and simmer for 8 minutes, stirring occasionally.

Stir in the black-eyed peas and the green beans, cover, and simmer for 10 minutes.

Preheat the oven to 350 degrees. Stir the rice into the vegetable mixture, cover, and bake for 30 to 40 minutes, checking to make sure there is enough liquid to prevent burning.

Yield: 8 servings

Heat Scale: Medium

Rich Food, Poor People

"My vegetarianism was anathema to all the people I met, and so was my aversion to rich, oily food. Meat and oil are a sign of wealth and respect, so I soon learned to accept plates of meat-covered rice swimming in palm oil with the gratitude such an offering deserved. I also quickly made friends with some hungry children who snuck off to the bush to finish my meal for me."

Ann C. Hudock

AROMATIC CHICKPEA TAJINE (TAJINE BIL HUMMUS)

Moroccan vegetable dishes are so good that they are sometimes served with rice or couscous for a light vegetarian meal. This particular recipe is aromatic with spices, and smells wonderful when it is cooking. Serve it with roasted lamb.

Another interesting way to serve this dish is as a filling for toasted pita bread—a Moroccan sandwich.

1½	pounds dried chickpeas	1	piece saffron thread (½ inch), crushed
3	tablespoons olive oil		
¾	cup grated onion, preferably red onion	2½	cups peeled, chopped tomatoes
2	fresh green chiles, such as jalapeños, seeds and stems removed, sliced	1	teaspoon salt
		¼	teaspoon freshly ground black pepper
½	teaspoon cumin powder	3	tablespoons chopped parsley
¾	teaspoon hot paprika	2	teaspoons chopped fresh cilantro
1	teaspoon freshly grated ginger		
½	teaspoon cinnamon		

Cover the chickpeas with water and soak overnight in the refrigerator.

Drain the chickpeas, rinse, place them in a large heavy casserole, and cover with water to 2 inches over the chickpeas. Bring the water to a boil, reduce the heat to a simmer, and simmer for at least 1 hour until they are tender. Drain well and set aside.

Heat the oil in a large skillet and sauté the onion and chiles for 1 minute. Add the cumin, paprika, ginger, cinnamon, and saffron, and sauté for 1 minute. Stir in the tomatoes, salt, pepper, parsley, cilantro, and drained chickpeas.

Cover the skillet and gently simmer for 15 to 20 minutes, stirring once or twice.

Yield: 6 servings

Heat Scale: Medium

Finger Food in North Africa

"Food is traditionally eaten with the thumb, forefinger, and middle finger of the right hand (the left hand is considered unclean); to eat with one finger is considered a sign of hatred, to eat with two shows pride, three accords with the Prophet Mohammed, while to eat with four or five fingers is a sign of gluttony."

Hilaire Walden

MIXED VEGETABLE TAJINE

In Chapter 5, you will find several recipes for *tajines* containing meat. However, this recipe is a vegetable stew that can be served with rice or couscous.

1 cup dry chickpeas	1 teaspoon salt
2 tablespoons olive oil	¼ teaspoon freshly ground black pepper
2 cups chopped onion	2½ cups chicken stock or vegetable stock
2 cloves garlic, minced	
1 cup sliced carrots	½ cup raisins
2 fresh green chiles, such as jalapeños, seeds and stems removed, sliced	Juice of one fresh lemon
1 cup sliced zucchini	¼ cup chopped scallions, white part only
2 cups chopped tomatoes	2 tablespoons chopped fresh cilantro
1 teaspoon ground cumin	

Soak the chickpeas overnight in the refrigerator.

Drain and rinse the chickpeas, place them in a large, heavy casserole, cover with cold water, bring the water to a boil, and cook the chickpeas until tender, about 1 hour. The cooking time depends on the age of the chickpeas, as well as the altitude in your area. Drain the chickpeas, chop them coarsely, and set aside.

Heat the oil in a large, heavy skillet and sauté the onion, garlic, carrots, chiles, and zucchini for 3 minutes. Add the tomatoes, cumin, salt, and pepper, and simmer for 2 minutes.

Add the stock and the raisins, and bring the mixture to a boil. Add the chopped chickpeas to the boiling mixture, reduce the heat to a simmer, cover, and simmer for 25 minutes.

Stir in the lemon juice, scallions, and cilantro, and serve.

Yield: 4 to 6 servings

Heat Scale: Mild

CHILE COCONUT RICE

This very popular and delicious side dish from Kenya and Tanzania is easy to make and easy to eat. It complements the flavor of chicken, curry dishes, or any kind of fish or seafood. Just make sure that you buy unsweetened coconut milk, rather than the sweetened variety that is used for bar drinks.

2   cups unsweetened coconut milk

1   cup white rice

1   teaspoon salt

¼   teaspoon freshly ground white pepper

½   cup chopped New Mexican green chiles, seeds and stems removed and excess moisture blotted out

Bring the coconut milk to a rolling boil, add the rice, salt, pepper, and chiles. Stir the mixture to blend, cover, reduce the heat to a simmer, and cook for 20 minutes.

Yield: 4 servings

Heat Scale: Medium

Cultural Uses of Rice

When a Cape Malay woman moves into a new house, the first items she carries with her over the threshold are three small containers: one filled with rice, one with sugar, and one with salt. She places these containers in the back of her cupboards until the family moves. The rice ensures that her cabinets will never be empty and the sugar that the household will be filled with sweetness; the salt keeps away evil spirits.

KOSHARY

Our friend, world traveler Richard Sterling, collected this recipe for us in Egypt. He wrote on the back of a risqué postcard: "*Koshary* is the most common Egyptian street food. It is ubiquitous, and the streets of Cairo are alive with its savor. The best example is to be found at Koshary Khadewi, a small restaurant immediately around the corner from the Stella Bar. An authentic Egyptian recipe for this dish would take up pages. Therefore I have taken liberties with Chef Gabriel Khalid's version so that busy people can enjoy this wonderful dish at home. Leftovers keep very well in a sealed container and make a good lunch or snack."

Layer 1
2   cups cooked rice, or rice with vermicelli (any flavor of Rice-a-Roni works well)

Layer 2
2   cups cooked elbow macaroni

Layer 3
1   cup cooked lentils

Layer 4
1   cup spicy tomato sauce, meatless spaghetti sauce, or salsa picante of your choice

Layer 5
3   large yellow onions, sliced thin and fried in oil until very brown and toasty (very important)

Layer 6
1   cup cooked garbanzo beans

Garlic-Vinegar Sauce
6   cloves garlic, mashed
¼   cup white vinegar
½   cup water
2   tablespoons lemon juice
1   teaspoon cumin
1   pinch salt

200

Combine all ingredients for the sauce in a glass jar. Cover and shake well.

Hot Pepper Sauce
Use any recipe from Chapter 2.

On a serving platter or plate, pile on each layer successively.
 Sprinkle with the garlic-vinegar sauce and the hot pepper sauce. Garnish with parsley.

Yield: 6 to 8 servings

Heat Scale: Varies

Monkey Bread

The baobab tree, native to tropical Africa, has a huge trunk that can be up to thirty feet wide. They are sometimes hollowed out and used as huts. But the real value of the tree is its large, edible, gourd-like fruit called "monkey bread." The fruit is eaten like a vegetable or is crushed and strained to make a refreshing drink.

SPICED GLAZED CARROTS WITH DILL

The spice in this South African vegetable side dish comes from a big dollop of fresh ginger. It is particularly good when it is served with any type of roasted fowl. Watch it carefully toward the end of the cooking time so that the carrots don't burn; you may have to sprinkle in a few drops of water.

4	cups carrots, sliced ¼ inch in diameter	⅓	cup butter
2	tablespoons honey	2	teaspoons grated orange zest
1	tablespoon freshly grated ginger	3	tablespoons fresh orange juice
1	jalapeño chile, seeds and stem removed, minced	2	teaspoons dried dill weed
		1	teaspoon salt
		¼	teaspoon freshly ground white pepper

Place all of the ingredients in a heavy, nonstick saucepan and barely cover with water. Bring the mixture to a boil, then reduce the heat to a simmer and cook for 10 to 12 minutes, until the carrots are just tender and the water has evaporated.

Yield: 6 servings

Heat Scale: Medium

SPICY WEST AFRICAN OKRA

This side dish is hot and spicy and would go well with one of the less spicy meat dishes. It can be served hot or chilled.

1	pound large, fresh okra	¼	teaspoon freshly ground black pepper
¾	cup minced onion		
3	cloves garlic, minced	2	teaspoons cayenne
1	teaspoon salt	6	cups water

Wash the okra, remove stems, and cut each into 3 pieces. Set aside.

In a large saucepan, mix together the onion, garlic, salt, pepper, cayenne, and the water. Bring the mixture to a boil, add the okra, reduce the heat to a simmer, and cook for 15 to 20 minutes.

Drain the mixture in a colander, rinse quickly with water, and serve.

Yield: 4 servings

Heat Scale: Medium

The Husband-Enhancing Greens

West Africans use a bewildering array of leaves, wild and cultivated, in cooking. Ghana alone boasts forty-seven edible kinds. Good housewives collect quantities in season, dry them, and store them for later use. The Yorubas of Nigeria call one kind of spinach *sokoyokoto,* meaning "make husband robust and fresh," which seems to be the way West Africans feel about all their vitamin-rich greens.

STEAMED CHILE CORN (IKPAKPALA)

This delicious Nigerian side dish has its fair share of heat, with the addition of both red and green hot chiles. It makes a good accompaniment for meat dishes, and it is especially good with roasted chicken or beef.

2	cups fresh corn kernels	1	tablespoon vegetable oil
1	medium onion, quartered	1	teaspoon salt
2	fresh hot green chiles, such as jalapeños, seeds and stems removed	¼	teaspoon freshly ground white pepper

Place the corn, onion, and chiles in a food processor and pulse the mixture until it is finely blended. Stir in the oil, salt, and pepper.

Pour the mixture into a greased casserole and cover tightly with aluminum foil. Place the casserole in a steamer and cook for 1¼ hours.

Yield: 4 servings

Heat Scale: Hot

SPICED AND STEAMED YAMS (AMUYALE)

This Nigerian yam recipe is rather unusual because the yams end up having the consistency of a dumpling. It is a delicious addition to any meal, as well as being an unusual side dish.

4	pounds yams	¾	cup minced onion, excess moisture drained out
1	teaspoon salt		
½	teaspoon freshly ground white pepper	¼	teaspoon thyme
		2	teaspoons cayenne powder

Peel the yams and grate them into a sieve so that any excess moisture can drain off.

Place the grated yams into a ceramic bowl and add the salt, pepper, onion, thyme, and cayenne and toss the mixture.

Place 3 tablespoons of the mixture in the center of a 6-inch square of aluminum foil, bring the ends toward the center, forming a ball of the yam mixture. Repeat with the remaining mixture.

Place the yam balls in a vegetable steamer and steam for 25 minutes.

Yield: 4 servings

Heat Scale: Mild

SPICED BOILED YAMS (ISU)

In Nigeria, yams are often used instead of potatoes. Any way in which potatoes can be prepared and served, yams can be cooked that way as well. Yams are also added to soups and stews. Nigerians, with their love of hot and spicy food, would probably eat cooked yams just sprinkled with hot ground red pepper.

4 pounds yams	¼ cup melted butter
1 teaspoon salt	1 tablespoon ground red
2 cloves garlic	*piri-piri* chile, or cayenne
1 stick cinnamon	

Peel the yams and slice them ½ inch thick. Place them in a casserole, cover with water, and add the salt, garlic, and cinnamon. Bring the water to a boil, reduce the heat, and cook until tender, about 15 to 20 minutes.

Drain the yams and arrange them on a heated platter. Drizzle the butter over the top, sprinkle the yams with the chile powder, and serve.

Yield: 4 servings

Heat Scale: Medium

MASHED PUNGENT PUMPKIN

Pumpkin is very popular in Nigeria, but it is seldom eaten in the rest of West Africa. The Ibo people in Nigeria have incorporated pumpkin into their regular diet. This recipe would make a refreshing change from the usual yams with Thanksgiving turkey.

1	small pumpkin (1 to 1½ pounds)	¼	teaspoon freshly ground white pepper
1½	teaspoons salt	2	tablespoons butter or vegetable oil
1	teaspoon cayenne powder		

Cut the pumpkin into quarters and remove the fiber and seeds. Place the sections in a large casserole, cover the pumpkin with water, and add 1 teaspoon of the salt. Bring the water to a boil, then reduce the heat to a simmer and simmer the pumpkin until it is tender, about 25 to 35 minutes.

Preheat the oven to 350 degrees.

Drain the pumpkin and remove the pulp from the skin, placing the pulp in a ceramic bowl. Add the cayenne, the remaining ½ teaspoon of salt, the pepper, and the butter, and mash the pulp until it is smooth.

Place the mashed pulp in a small casserole dish, cover, and reheat in the oven for 15 minutes. Alternatively, you can form the pumpkin into 4 or 5 patties and sauté in the butter or oil.

Yield: 4 servings

Heat Scale: Medium

VEGETABLES IN PEANUT SAUCE

This is a West African side dish that can be served over rice as a vegetarian meal, or served as an accompaniment to a meat dish. Palm oil is a reddish oil extracted from the pulp of the fruit of the African palm; it has a distinct color and flavor, but because it is high in saturated fat we suggest using a vegetable oil.

1	tablespoon palm or vegetable oil	2	cups vegetable stock, boiled and reduced to 1 cup
1	cup chopped onion	¼	teaspoon allspice
3	cloves garlic, minced	1	teaspoon salt
¼	cup unsalted smooth peanut butter	2	carrots, sliced
		2	cups shredded white cabbage
3	pounds tomatoes peeled, seeded, and puréed	1	cup fresh okra, sliced into ½-inch pieces
3½	cups water	½	cup chopped red bell pepper
1	teaspoon thyme		
2	hot green chiles, such as jalapeños, seeds and stems removed, chopped		

Heat the oil in a large, heavy skillet, and sauté the onion and garlic for 3 minutes, stirring to prevent the garlic from burning. Stir in the peanut butter and the tomatoes and simmer for 1 minute.

Place 2 cups vegetable stock in a heavy saucepan and bring it to a boil. Lower the temperature to a simmer and cook until the stock is reduced to 1 cup.

In a small saucepan, add the water and the thyme, chiles, ⅓ cup reduced vegetable stock, allspice, and salt and bring the mixture to a boil. Reduce the heat to a simmer and simmer for 30 minutes, uncovered. Stir the mixture occasionally to make sure it doesn't burn. This is the sauce for the vegetables, and it should be just slightly thick.

Pour the remaining ⅔ cup of reduced stock into a medium-size saucepan and bring it to a boil. Add the carrots, cabbage, okra, and bell pepper, and reduce the heat to a simmer. Cook the vegetables until they are just barely tender.

Drain the vegetables and put them in a warm serving dish. Pour the sauce over the vegetables and serve immediately.

Yield: 4 servings

Heat Scale: Mild

What Vegetables to Eat in Africa
When You Run Out of Monkey Bread

- Air potatoes are the bulbils of yams that grow in the air rather than the dirt in tropical Africa. They are about the size of a man's thumb and are usually boiled.
- Crab grass and its seeds have been part of the African diet for centuries. The seeds can be eaten as a cereal or ground into flour.
- "Lady fingers" is an African and Asian term for okra, also called *gombo.*

FRIED PEPPERS WITH CAPERS AND GARLIC

This is a side dish that has big flavors and is very versatile. Because the chiles are fried until the skins are scorched, it gives a unique taste. Serve the dish hot as you would any other vegetable, or chill it and serve it as an appetizer.

¼ cup good-quality olive oil
1½ pounds fresh red New Mexican chiles, seeds and stems removed, cut into strips
5 cloves garlic, minced
2 tablespoons capers

2 tablespoons white wine vinegar or tarragon vinegar
½ teaspoon salt
¼ teaspoon freshly ground black pepper

Heat the oil in a large, heavy skillet until it is almost sizzling. Add the chiles and fry them, stirring constantly, until the skins are charred. Remove the chiles, cool slightly, and remove the skins.

Return the chiles to the hot skillet, add the garlic and capers, and sauté for 1 minute.

Stir in the vinegar, salt, and pepper, and allow the mixture to simmer until the moisture has evaporated.

Serve hot or cold or as an appetizer.

Variation: When you have completed the recipe, purée the mixture, add 2 tablespoons of sour cream or unflavored yogurt, and serve it as a spread on garlic toasts.

Yield: 6 servings

Heat Scale: Medium

ONION TAJINE

Another delicious vegetarian *tajine* from North Africa, this one is particularly good when it is served with grilled meats or poultry. Red onions are preferred when they are used in *tajines*. The cinnamon and saffron add an exotic flavor to this dish.

2 teaspoons crushed, dried, hot red chile	¼ teaspoon crushed saffron
2 teaspoons coarsely crushed black pepper	1 teaspoon salt
¼ cup ground cinnamon	2 pounds red onions, peeled and sliced into ¼-inch slices
1 teaspoon ground ginger	½ cup good-quality olive oil
3 tablespoons sugar	4 celery stalks, cut 8 inches long

Mix together the chile, pepper, cinnamon, ginger, 2 tablespoons of the sugar, saffron, and salt, and set ⅓ of the mixture aside.

Layer the sliced onions and the remaining ⅔ of the spice mix in a ceramic pan and pour the olive oil over the top. Allow the mixture to marinate at room temperature for at least 2 hours.

Preheat the oven to 325 degrees.

Arrange the celery in a crisscross fashion in the bottom of a heavy, ovenproof casserole. Add the marinated onion mixture, sprinkle the reserved spice mix and the remaining sugar over the top. Cover the casserole and bake for 40 minutes. If desired, remove the cover and brown the top of the mixture lightly under a broiler.

Serve immediately.

Yield: 4 to 5 servings

Heat Scale: Mild

FRESH TOMATO AND GREEN CHILE RELISH (TEEMATEEM BEQARYA)

This Ethiopian relish is not only hot and spicy, but it is served chilled, so your taste buds get a double thrill. This recipe is similar to a Southwestern salsa. However, instead of tortilla chips, *Injera* Bread (see recipe, p. 217) is served with this relish.

¾	cup chopped, roasted, peeled New Mexican green chiles	½	teaspoon salt
3	cups peeled chopped tomatoes	1½	tablespoons fresh lemon or lime juice
3	tablespoons vegetable oil	¼	teaspoon freshly ground black pepper
⅓	cup chopped red onions		

Toss all of the ingredients together in a medium-size ceramic bowl. Cover and marinate at room temperature for 1 hour.

Refrigerate the mixture for 2 hours and then serve.

Yield: 6 servings

Heat Scale: Medium

HOT AFRICAN GREENS AND BEEF (SUKUMA WIKI)

Sukuma Wiki is a green leafy vegetable. This tasty and simple side dish goes well with any type of meat or fish main course. Since it is only lightly spiced, we suggest you serve it with one of the more highly seasoned recipes for fish, chicken, or meat.

1	pound *Sukuma Wiki,* or kale, spinach, or turnip greens, washed well	1	teaspoon salt
3	tablespoons vegetable oil	¼	teaspoon freshly ground black pepper
1	cup chopped onion	½	cup chopped leftover meat
2	cups chopped tomatoes		*Piri-piri* sherry (optional) (see recipe, p. 221)
1	jalapeño chile, seeds and stem removed, chopped		

Dry the greens and shred them very finely.

Heat the oil in a large skillet and sauté the onion for 3 minutes. Add the tomatoes, chile, salt, pepper, and shredded greens. Toss the mixture in the skillet, cover, and simmer for 10 minutes.

Remove the cover, add the meat, and simmer uncovered for 10 to 15 minutes, until the greens are tender. Check periodically to prevent burning.

If you wish, *piri-piri* sherry may be sprinkled on top for extra flavor when the vegetable is served.

Yield: 4 servings

Heat Scale: Mild

DRIED FRUIT CURRY

This South African recipe shows the influence the East had on African cooking. It is one of many recipes using dried fruits, rice, and spices that were brought from the East to Africa by traders. Serve this dish with lamb.

¼ cup chopped dates
¼ cup chopped prunes
½ cup raisins
1 cup dried apples
2 cups water
2 tablespoons vegetable oil
1 cup chopped onion

3 tablespoons Malawi Curry Power (see recipe, p. 14)
2 tablespoons lemon juice
2 tablespoons red wine vinegar
2 bananas, sliced
¼ cup chopped, salted peanuts

Place the dates, prunes, raisins, and apples in a small, heavy saucepan and add the water. Bring the mixture to a boil, reduce the heat quickly to a simmer, and cook for 45 minutes. Stir the mixture occasionally to prevent burning.

Heat the oil in a skillet and sauté the onions for 3 minutes, until the onion starts to wilt. Add the curry powder, cooked fruit, lemon juice, and vinegar and simmer for 2 minutes to allow the flavors to blend. If the mixture looks too dry, add a few tablespoons of water.

Place the fruit on a small platter, surround it with the bananas, and sprinkle with the chopped nuts.

Yield: 4 servings

Heat Scale: Medium

FRIKKADEL CURRY

This well-known South African curry dish is usually served as an accompaniment to roasted meats. Hot, cooked white rice is also served on the side with this dish.

3	tablespoons vegetable oil	2	teaspoons Malawi Curry Powder (see recipe, p. 14)
2	cups coarsely chopped onion	2	bay leaves
4	cloves garlic, minced	¼	cup water
2	jalapeño chiles, seeds and stems removed, chopped	¾	pound minced beef
1	cup peeled, chopped tomato	1	beaten egg
½	teaspoon turmeric	½	teaspoon freshly ground pepper
½	teaspoon salt	¼	teaspoon nutmeg
½	teaspoon cumin	½	teaspoon cinnamon
1	teaspoon ground coriander		

Heat the oil in a large skillet and sauté the onion for 3 minutes. Add half the garlic, the chiles, tomato, turmeric, salt, cumin, coriander, curry powder, bay leaves, and the water. Cover the mixture and simmer for 15 minutes, stirring once or twice.

While the onion mixture is simmering, combine the beef, egg, pepper, the remaining garlic, nutmeg, and cinnamon in a medium bowl. Form the mixture into 1½-inch balls and add them to the simmered mixture. Cover and continue simmering for 20 minutes more.

Remove the bay leaves before serving.

Variation: Add 1 cup unflavored yogurt to the mixture 15 minutes before the end of the cooking time.

Yield: 6 servings

Heat Scale: Mild

PERI-PERI PEANUT MUFFINS

This delicious West African bread contains both chile and peanuts and is baked in muffin tins. The muffins freeze well, and are particularly good when they are served warm.

½	cup butter	½	cup milk
½	teaspoon salt	1	teaspoon baking powder
1	teaspoon *peri-peri* chile powder, or cayenne	1½	cups all-purpose flour
¼	cup sugar	¾	cup finely chopped unsalted, roasted peanuts
2	eggs, lightly beaten		

Preheat the oven to 400 degrees.

Cream the butter, salt, chile powder, and sugar until the mixture is light; mix in the eggs and milk.

Sift the baking powder and the flour together. Add to the creamed mixture and stir until the ingredients are blended. Stir in ½ cup of the peanuts.

Fill greased muffin tins about ⅓ full and sprinkle the tops of the muffins with the remaining peanuts. Bake for 12 minutes.

Serve the muffins hot with honey drizzled over the top.

Yield: 12 large or 18 medium muffins
Heat Scale: Mild

216

INJERA BREAD (YESINDE INJERA)

This bread is one of the few we know of that is utilized as a bread, as silverware, and as placemats. One of the many places we ate this bread was at the Blue Nile Restaurant in New York. Traditionally, a large tray is covered with concentric circles of Injera, and the different selections of food are piled on top of each circle. Pieces of the bread are then broken off and used to scoop up the food. Additional pieces of bread are served on the side. Often the batter is allowed to ferment to make sourdough *Injera*.

4½	cups self-rising flour	2	cups unflavored club soda
½	cup whole wheat flour	4	cups water
1	teaspoon baking powder		

Mix the two flours with the baking powder. Add the club soda and the water, and stir the batter until it is smooth and rather thin.

Heat a large nonstick skillet (10 or 12 inches in diameter) until a drop of water bounces in the bottom of the pan.

Measure out about ¾ cup of the batter, tip the pan slightly, and quickly pour the batter into the pan. Cook the *Injera* until small holes appear on the surface, then remove it from the pan. The bread should appear slightly moist when done. *Injera* is only cooked on one side.

Stack the bread rounds on top of each other as they are removed from the pan and cover them with a light towel.

Yield: 4 to 6 servings

ROTI BREAD

Roti (the Hindi word for bread) is of Indian origin and is cooked on a griddle. Sometimes baking powder is omitted, which makes the bread very thin. We suggest you try both methods and see which one you like the best.

3   cups flour
1   tablespoon baking powder
½   teaspoon salt

1   cup water
Vegetable oil

Sift together the flour, baking powder, and salt. Add the water and mix to form a dough. Knead for 3 minutes, cover, and allow the bread to stand for 30 minutes. Knead again, divide the dough into four sections, and then form each section into a ball.

On a floured board, roll out each ball as thin as possible, to a diameter of 8 to 10 inches.

Heat a large skillet and coat it with oil. Add one of the rotis, and cook for 1 minute per side, adding more oil onto each side as it cooks. Remove and drain on paper towels. Repeat the process for the remaining balls. The balls should appear cooked (not sticky) when done.

Yield: 4 large rotis

Bunny Chow

"South African Bunny Chow is not a feast for rabbits, as the name might imply. Instead, this hearty, spicy, economical meal precedes the Big Mac as one of the original fast foods that even comes in its own biodegradable package. A bunny, which is a hollowed-out loaf of bread filled with beans, spices and gravy, should be eaten whilst walking or sitting on pavement or grass."

Nick Zehnder

Herbs, Spices, Fruits, and Nuts: African Drinks and Desserts

After all the heat in the previous chapters, here's a chance to finally cool down. Well, ginger does make an appearance in some of these recipes, but chiles do not. Unlike other regions of the world with chile-spiced drinks and desserts, Africa seems to like these dishes rich and flavorful, but heatless.

We begin with two herbally infused teas. Moroccan Mint Tea (p. 222) is a favorite in North Africa at virtually any time of the day or night, while the unusual Lemon Grass Tea (p. 223) is served primarily in West Africa. The word "beer" is a bit of a misnomer for African Ginger Beer (p. 224), as it is neither fermented nor alcoholic, but it's a favorite all over sub-Saharan Africa, where it makes a refreshing and tangy drink.

Our first party drink from Africa is the White Elephant (p. 225), which is the African version of a piña colada, without the piña (pineapple). Ethiopian Party Punch (p. 226) features five different fruit juices with an alcohol option, while Pineapple Cooler (p. 227) focuses on clove-spiced pineapple.

We conclude our drink selections with two unusual but delicious concoctions. Mombasa Coffee (p. 228) is infused with the flavors of cardamom, cinnamon, and cloves, while Nigerian Rice Water (p. 229) not only contains rice, but also cinnamon, nutmeg, and orange peel.

Our desserts begin with two sweet spreads. Almond Paste from Morocco (*Amalou,* p. 230) is an almond-and-honey spread for hot breads, while East African Banana Jam (p. 231) makes an excellent topping for cakes and rolls. The jam introduces our banana desserts, followed by West African Baked Bananas (p. 232), flavored with lime juice and brown sugar, and the very rich Frozen Banana Cream (p. 233) from Tanzania.

Another fruit recipe from the same country is Tanzanian Pineapple and Nut Salad (p. 234), with cashews and coconut complementing the pineapple. A medley of fruits is utilized in Fruit Fritters (p. 235), which are simply battered and deep-fried sections of banana, pineapple, papaya, and orange. Oranges also play a key role in Orange-Coconut Pudding (p. 236), a dessert from Liberia that can be served with breads or cakes. Why not try it with another dessert from the same country, Liberian Pumpkin Cake (p. 237)?

Twisted Caraway Cakes (*Chinchin,* p. 238), a tasty Nigerian pastry that's also a street food, are easy to make. Our final two cakes include our third Liberian dessert, Liberian Plantain Gingerbread (p. 240), which is spiced with cinnamon and cloves as well as ginger. And speaking of ginger, our Ginger

Cake (p. 239) utilizes both powdered and crystallized ginger for an added tangy flavor in this Nigerian cake.

We conclude our desserts with four North African specialties. As we know, nuts are beloved in the region, so Almond-Sesame Pastries (p. 242) and Algerian Almond Cookies (p. 243) feature the almond along with spices such cinnamon, sesame, and orange-flower water. Gazelle's Horns (*Tcharak*, p. 244) are an Algerian sweet croissant, while Walnut "Sandwich" Candies (p. 245) are a popular Tunisian dessert.

Secrets of *Piri-Piri* Sherry

"This is a delicious and handy condiment common in Anglo-Kenyan households. A large bottle or jar (old Lea & Perrins bottles or hot-sauce bottles with shaker caps are ideal) is filled with fresh *piquin*-type chiles. Pour over dry sherry to cover, close bottle, and let sit for at least three weeks. Use as you would use pepper vinegar on spinach or greens, or add a dash to your soups. You can even use it for a hot sherry vinaigrette! As sherry is used, top up occasionally, using only a small amount or you'll get too much of a raw sherry taste. There are families whose sherry has been topped up continuously for 20 years, and they claim it is still hot, but I find that the chiles lose their potency after about one year. If you like this combination, try it with other chiles, like habaneros."

Michelle Cox, Driftwood Beach Club, Malindi, Kenya

MOROCCAN MINT TEA

This tea is served all over North Africa and is particularly favored in Morocco. The theory goes that the British brought tea to North Africa, where it quickly became popular with the addition of sugar and mint leaves. Feel free to alter the amounts of the ingredients to suit your taste.

2 teaspoons green or gunpowder tea	Fresh spearmint sprigs
⅓ cup sugar	3 cups boiling water

Put the tea, sugar, and mint sprigs in a teapot. Cover with the boiling water and allow to steep for 3 to 4 minutes before serving.

Yield: 3 cups

LEMON GRASS TEA

Herb teas are very popular in West Africa. This one, a favorite in Liberia and Sierra Leone, is made with the slender blades of wild lemon grass. Fresh lemon grass is available in Asian markets and natural food supermarkets. Try this tea with any of the rich desserts in this chapter.

1	cup chopped lemon grass leaves	Sugar (optional)
2	cups boiling water	Milk (optional)

Place the lemon grass leaves in a teapot and pour the boiling water over them. Steep for about 5 minutes.

Serve with sugar and milk, if desired.

Yield: 2 cups

Now That's Aged Wine

"The Egyptians, who crushed grapes in large canvas bags, twisting them with sticks, made careful notes on their jars of the date when the wine inside had been made, its type and color, and the names of the vineyard and the wine-grower. Sealed wines have been found in tombs which are equally carefully dated—and some of these wines were over two centuries old when they were put in the tombs; the dead took samples of the best of their household goods with them."

Maguelonne Toussaint-Samat

AFRICAN GINGER BEER

This drink is popular in sub-Saharan Africa, and especially in Sierra Leone and Ghana. It is made with varying ratios of water to ginger, and many different fruits, including pineapple and guava, which can be substituted for the citrus in this recipe. This recipe makes a strong concentrate that can be diluted with equal parts of water for drinking, but many people like it as strong as this undiluted recipe.

16	ounces fresh ginger, washed and peeled	1	stick cinnamon
2	quarts boiling water	1	teaspoon whole cloves
	Juice of 2 limes	1	cup sugar

Grind or pound the ginger to a pulp, and place in a large ceramic or glass jar. Cover with the boiling water and place the mixture in a warm place.

After 1 hour, strain the liquid through cheesecloth, squeezing the pulp to extract all the flavor. Stir in the lime juice, cinnamon, cloves, and sugar. Let the liquid sit for another hour, in the sun if possible.

Strain again through cheesecloth, transfer the ginger beer to another jar, and refrigerate.

Yield: ½ gallon

WHITE ELEPHANT

This is a favorite alcoholic drink in the Congo Republic. It is rich and fatty because it contains coconut milk, so be forewarned!

2   cups coconut milk
2   tablespoons sugar
¾   cup white rum
¾   cup white Creme de Cacao

1   cup crushed ice, plus extra for serving
Freshly grated nutmeg for garnish

Place all ingredients, minus the nutmeg, in a blender and process until smooth. Place a tablespoon of crushed ice in a glass, pour the drink over it, and garnish with nutmeg.

Yield: About 4 cups

Call It Elephant Brew

"Except among Moslems, homemade beer is the traditional relaxing or social drink throughout Africa. Herding peoples use wild honey or grain acquired by trading to make their brew; in grain-growing areas, it is made with corn, sorghum, or millet; in the rain forests, mashed bananas are the base. In some places, special trees or plants peculiar to the area provide the makings for the beer. One such is the Maroela tree that grows in northern Southwest Africa, yielding tons and tons of a small, apple-looking fruit. It isn't only the people who prize the Maroela fruit. In season, when the fruit falls to the ground and begins to ferment, it is relished by elephants who become quite drunk on it and can become dangerous."

Harva Hachten

ETHIOPIAN PARTY PUNCH

This is a refreshing drink that helps to cool down those very hot Ethiopian meals that are spiced up with *Berbere* (see recipe, p. 25). This recipe makes enough punch for a large party. Some hosts add a half-quart of vodka to this mixture to further enliven the party.

1	cup orange juice	1	cup raspberry syrup
1	cup lemon juice	2½	quarts club soda
1	cup pineapple juice		Fresh mint leaves for garnish
2	cups white grape juice		

Combine all ingredients in the order given in a large punch bowl. Garnish with the mint leaves.

Yield: 1 gallon

PINEAPPLE COOLER

Here's another party favorite, this time from Ghana. Try this accompanied by some of the appetizers from Chapter 3. Again, some hosts add vodka or gin to really liven up the party.

1	fresh pineapple		Sugar to taste
3	whole cloves		Ice cubes
	Peelings from half an orange	1	sprig fresh mint for garnish
1	quart boiling water		

Slice the skin off the pineapple and save the peels. Chop 1 cup of the pineapple fruit for use.

Place the pineapple peelings and fruit, cloves, and orange peelings into a bowl or jar. Add the boiling water, cover, and let stand for 24 hours. Strain though a strainer or cheesecloth. Sweeten with sugar as desired.

Pour over ice cubes and serve with a sprig of fresh mint on top.

Yield: 1 quart

MOMBASA COFFEE

Coffee, which is grown in many parts of Africa, is considerably spiced up in Kenya. This version can also be prepared by adding the cardamom, cinnamon, and cloves to the basket of an automatic coffee brewer.

3	cardamom pods, unhusked	2	cups water
2	sticks cinnamon	5	teaspoons freshly ground coffee
4	cloves		

Boil the cardamom, cinnamon, and cloves in the water in a pot for 10 minutes. Add the coffee and boil 5 minutes longer. Pour into a serving pot, but do not strain the spices. Allow to stand until the grounds settle, then pour into small cups.

Yield: 2 cups or 4 servings

Beer of the Goddess

"The ancient Egyptians were obsessed with beer—it anointed the newborn baby, was minimum wage for a day's work, and went into the tomb with the dead. The Nile dwellers even wrote the word 'food' as a loaf of bread and a pitcher of beer. Non-alcoholic beers also came from old Egypt. The daughters of Hathor would brew a potent beer that was taken into the temple and heated over fire, the alcohol or 'spirit' of the beer rising to the heavens and making the goddess quite drunk. The remaining now non-alcoholic brew was sold to the public, the proceeds going in support of the temple."

Alan Eames

NIGERIAN RICE WATER

This unusual drink is served for either breakfast or dessert in Nigeria. It is particularly popular in Lagos.

1 tablespoon rice
2 cups whole milk
1 teaspoon sugar
⅛ teaspoon ground cinnamon

⅛ teaspoon ground nutmeg
⅛ teaspoon grated orange or lemon peel

Place the rice into a pan with the milk and bring to a boil. Reduce the heat and simmer for 30 minutes. Strain through cheesecloth and add the sugar, cinnamon, nutmeg, and peel. Chill in the refrigerator and serve.

Yield: 2 cups

ALMOND PASTE FROM MOROCCO (AMALOU)

This is a well-known delicacy from the Souss region in southwest Morocco. *Amalou* is served with hot baked or fried bread, or used as a filling for pancakes.

1 teaspoon vegetable oil	Salt to taste
1½ cups blanched almonds	¼ cup thick honey
½ cup walnut oil	

Heat a little vegetable oil in a pan, then add the almonds and brown. Drain on paper towels then process them in a blender with the walnut oil and salt until smooth and creamy. Add the honey and process briefly until well blended.

Pour into a jar, cover, and keep in the refrigerator. The paste should then keep for at least 2 months.

Try with *Peri-Peri* Peanut Muffins (see recipe, p. 216)

Yield: About 1¼ cups

EAST AFRICAN BANANA JAM

Bananas are common on both sides of the African continent. This jam is great to spread on bread or toast. It's also used as a topping for cakes.

2   cups sugar
½   cup lemon juice
1   tablespoon lemon zest

6   ripe medium bananas, peeled and sliced into ½-inch rounds

In a large nonmetallic bowl, stir together the sugar, lemon juice, and lemon zest until the sugar dissolves. Fold in the banana slices until they are evenly coated. Cover the bowl with plastic wrap or foil and let the bananas marinate at room temperature for at least 1 hour.

Place the bananas and marinade in a saucepan. Bring to a boil, stirring frequently to break up the bananas. Reduce the heat to very low and simmer, uncovered, for 30 minutes, stirring occasionally. The jam should be very thick. Immediately ladle the jam into an airtight container and refrigerate.

Yield: About 3 cups

WEST AFRICAN BAKED BANANAS

Since bananas are ubiquitous in West African cuisine, it is not unusual at all to find them in desserts. In fact, they could be served in every course of a meal.

4 large bananas, ripe but firm	¼ cup heavy cream
2 teaspoons lime juice	Crushed peanuts for garnish
2 teaspoons brown sugar	

Heat the oven to 350 degrees. Place the unpeeled bananas on a baking sheet or in a shallow pan. Bake for 20 minutes, until the skins are brown.

Remove the bananas to serving plates. Make two slits along the length of each banana and pull back and remove a strip of the peel to reveal the banana. Squeeze ½ teaspoon of lime juice over each fruit, then sprinkle with brown sugar. Ladle a tablespoon of cream over each fruit. Garnish with the crushed peanuts.

Yield: 4 servings

FROZEN BANANA CREAM

This Tanzanian recipe is yet another example of the many uses of bananas in Africa. This is a vanilla-egg custard which is mixed with whipped cream, superfine sugar, mashed bananas, and flavoring, and then frozen.

Egg Custard
1   cup milk
2   eggs

2   tablespoons superfine sugar
2   to 3 drops vanilla extract

Heat the milk almost to the boiling point, but do not let it boil. Break the eggs into the hot milk, add the sugar and vanilla essence, and whisk to a creamy mixture. Simmer slowly on very low heat, stirring continuously until it thickens into a smooth custard. Remove from the heat and set aside.

Banana Cream
2   very ripe bananas, thoroughly mashed

1   tablespoon sugar
1   cup cream, whipped
    Banana rounds for garnish

Mix together thoroughly the egg custard, mashed bananas, and sugar. Blend in the whipped cream. Transfer into a serving dish and freeze.

Decorate and serve with fresh banana cut into rounds.

Yield: 4 servings

233

TANZANIAN PINEAPPLE AND NUT SALAD

Fresh fruit served alone or in a combination salad is the most typical ending to an African's meal. Feel free to add bananas or other tropical fruits to this dessert from Tanzania in East Africa.

2	cups pineapple cubes	½	cup light cream
4	heaping tablespoons grated coconut	2	tablespoons honey
2	heaping tablespoons cashew nuts	⅓	cup white rum or banana liqueur

In a bowl, combine the pineapple, coconut, and cashews. Add the cream, honey, and rum. Mix well and let stand for 1 hour at room temperature. Refrigerate and serve cool.

Yield: 4 servings

FRUIT FRITTERS

A very popular dessert in West Africa is made by dipping pieces of fruit in batter and deep-frying them. While still hot, they often are sprinkled with sugar. They are usually served with a wedge of lemon or lime.

1	egg yolk	1	egg white	
⅓	cup water		Peanut oil for frying	
2	teaspoons vegetable oil	1	cup sliced bananas	
1	teaspoon lime or lemon juice	1	cup cubed pineapple	
½	cup flour	1	cup cubed papaya	
1	tablespoon sugar	1	cup orange segments	
⅛	plus ¼ teaspoon salt			

With a wire whisk, beat the egg yolk and water. Add the oil and lime or lemon juice, blending thoroughly.

Sift the flour, sugar, and the ⅛ teaspoon of salt together, and combine the liquid and the dry ingredients. Add the remaining ¼ teaspoon of salt to the egg white and beat until it forms stiff peaks. Fold the egg white into the original mixture.

Heat the oil in a deep pan. Using tongs, dip the pieces of fruit in the batter and drop into the hot oil. Cook until the batter turns light brown. Remove and drain on paper towels.

Serve a mixed plate of fruit at room temperature.

Yield: 4 servings

ORANGE-COCONUT PUDDING

Here is an easy-to-make fruit pudding from Liberia, in West Africa. Try serving it with Mombasa Coffee (see recipe, p. 228) for a truly unique ending to an African meal.

2	cups milk	¼	teaspoon salt
2	tablespoons butter or margarine		Grated rind of 2 medium oranges
1	cup dry bread crumbs, firmly packed	1¼	cups grated coconut (fresh preferred)
2	egg yolks	2	egg whites
⅓	cup, plus ¼ cup sugar	¼	teaspoon cream of tartar

Heat the milk to just below boiling point. Add the butter and crumbs and let stand.

Beat the egg yolks, add ⅓ cup of the sugar, the salt, and half the grated rind. Add the grated coconut to the egg yolk mixture, then add the milk mixture and blend.

Preheat the oven to 300 degrees. Fill greased custard cups about two-thirds full with the mixture. Bake for about 40 minutes, or until firm and very lightly browned.

Beat the egg whites with the cream of tartar until they are frothy. Gradually add the remaining ¼ cup of sugar, a spoonful at a time, beating until the meringue is stiff and glossy. Add the rest of rind.

Remove the pudding cups from the oven and spread the meringue over each. Increase the oven heat to 400 degrees, return the baked puddings to oven, and bake for about 8 minutes or until the meringue is set and lightly browned.

Yield: 6 to 8 servings

LIBERIAN PUMPKIN CAKE

Another West African recipe from Liberia, this dessert uses the popular pumpkin. Top it with your favorite icing.

½	cup butter or margarine	½	teaspoon nutmeg
1¼	cups sugar	½	teaspoon salt
2	eggs	1	cup canned pumpkin
2	cups sifted all-purpose flour	¾	cup milk
1	tablespoon baking powder	½	teaspoon baking soda
½	teaspoon cinnamon		

Preheat the oven to 350 degrees. Cream the butter, add the sugar, and blend the two together thoroughly. Beat the eggs and add them to the butter, mixing well.

Sift together the flour, baking powder, spices, and salt. In a separate bowl, mix the pumpkin with the milk and baking soda. Add the dry and liquid ingredients alternately to the egg mixture, blending the batter well.

Bake in two greased layer pans for about 25 minutes, or until the cake tests done. Let it cool in the pans for a few minutes, then turn out on a cake rack to cool before frosting.

Yield: 6 to 8 servings

TWISTED CARAWAY CAKES (CHINCHIN)

These crisp, slightly sweet knots of pastry are often sold by street vendors in Nigeria along the roads or at railroad stations. Try them with Tanzanian Pineapple and Nut Salad (see recipe, p. 234).

2   tablespoons butter
1   cup all-purpose flour
2   tablespoons sugar
1   teaspoon caraway seed, or
    nutmeg, anise seed, or
    grated orange rind

1   egg, beaten
    Vegetable oil for deep-frying

Mix the butter thoroughly into the flour. Add the sugar and caraway seed and mix well. Mix in the beaten egg, forming a stiff dough. A few drops of water may be added if needed, but the dough should be kept firm. Knead until smooth or use a bread machine for kneading.

Roll out the dough on a floured board to a thin sheet. Cut into strips about ½- to ¾-inch wide and 4 to 5 inches long, with angled ends. With a knife point, make a small slit just left of center and slip the right-hand end through it, forming a half-bow.

Heat the oil to 350 to 375 degrees. Fry the knots, turning to brown evenly. Drain on paper towels.

Yield: 3 dozen pieces

GINGER CAKE

Another Nigerian favorite uses two types of prepared ginger—dried ground and crystallized. Serve this crusty cake with vanilla ice cream for a complete sweet dessert.

2	cups flour	1	egg, beaten	
1½	teaspoons baking powder	⅝	cup milk	
½	teaspoon baking soda	1	tablespoon ground ginger	
½	teaspoon salt	¼	cup chopped crystallized ginger	
½	cup sugar			
¾	cup molasses			
6	tablespoons butter or margarine			

Preheat the oven to 325 degrees. Sift the flour, baking powder, baking soda, and salt together. Set aside.

Mix the sugar, molasses, and butter together in a saucepan and heat until the sugar melts and the whole is nicely liquid but not too hot.

Mix the beaten egg and milk together. Add the heated mixture slowly to the egg and milk. Stir in the dry ingredients, mixing well. Fold in the two kinds of ginger.

Bake in a greased 9-inch loaf or round cake pan for about 50 minutes, or until it tests done. Allow to cool slightly in the pan, then turn it out on cake rack to finish cooling.

Yield: 6 to 8 servings

LIBERIAN PLANTAIN GINGERBREAD

This is an African upside-down cake. Two firm bananas can be substituted for the plantain. If you use bananas, they should not be precooked. Plantains can be found in Latin markets.

½   cup sugar
½   cup water
2   cups sliced half-ripe plantain
2⅓ cups all-purpose flour
½   teaspoon salt
1½ teaspoons baking soda
1   teaspoon ground ginger
1   teaspoon ground cinnamon

¼   teaspoon ground cloves
¼   teaspoon ground nutmeg
⅓   cup butter or margarine, plus extra for coating cake pan
1   cup molasses
⅔   cup boiling water
     Whipped cream for garnish

Preheat the oven to 350 degrees.

Mix the sugar with the ½ cup water in a saucepan over moderate heat, stirring until the sugar is dissolved. Bring to a boil.

Add the plantain to the boiling sugar syrup, and cook for about 5 minutes. Remove the plantain and drain.

Butter a 9-inch square cake pan heavily. Spread the plantain slices evenly over the bottom.

Sift together the flour, salt, baking soda, ginger, cinnamon, cloves, and nutmeg. Set aside.

Place the butter and molasses in a saucepan over moderate heat and bring to a boil. Remove from the heat. Pour in the boiling water and stir. Gradually add the sifted dry ingredients, stirring, and then beat vigorously. Pour the batter over the sliced plantain.

Bake for about 50 minutes, or until the cake tests done. Let the pan stand for 5 minutes on a rack, then loosen with a spatula and turn the cake upside down on a serving plate.

Cut into squares, top with whipped cream, and serve warm or cooled.

Yield: 6 to 8 servings

The African Culinary Legacy

"From Africa with the people in bondage came new foods: okra, black-eyed peas, collard greens, yams, sesame seed, and water-melons. From Central and South America, meanwhile—some-times through Europe and Africa and Asia—came hot and sweet peppers, peanuts, tomatoes, lima beans, chocolate, white potatoes, and sweet potatoes. Up from Florida came oranges and peaches, natives of China brought to the New World by the Spanish. The kitchen was one of the few places where the imagination and skill of blacks could have free rein and expres-sion, and there they often excelled. From the elegant breads and meats and sweets of plantation cookery to the inventive genius of Creole cuisine, from beaten biscuits to bouillabaisse, their legacy of culinary excellence is all the more impressive, considering the extremely adverse conditions under which it was compiled."

John Egerton

ALMOND-SESAME PASTRIES

Like all North African pastries, these from Tunisia are very sweet, and only one or two can be eaten at a time. Fortunately, they keep well when stored in an airtight container.

1¼ cups water	1½ teaspoons finely grated orange zest
⅔ cup sugar	1½ teaspoons ground cinnamon
1 tablespoon lemon juice	About 4 ounces phyllo pastry
1 tablespoon orange-flower water	Olive oil
1½ cups blanched almonds, lightly toasted and ground	Lightly toasted sesame seeds

Place the water and ½ cup of the sugar in a saucepan and heat gently, stirring until the sugar is dissolved. Add the lemon juice and boil until syrupy. Remove from the heat and add the orange-flower water. Allow to cool.

Preheat the oven to 350 degrees. In a mixing bowl, stir together the ground almonds, orange zest, cinnamon, and remaining sugar, then knead together.

Brush one sheet of phyllo with olive oil; keep the other sheets covered with a damp cloth. Cut the oiled sheet into 3 strips lengthwise. Place a small spoonful of filling at the bottom of each strip.

Fold the sides over the filling then roll the pastry up along its length. Brush inside the end of the pastry with oil and seal it to the roll. Brush with oil and place on a baking sheet. Repeat with the remaining pastry and filling. Bake the pastries for 15 to 20 minutes until crisp and golden.

Lower the pastries a few at a time into the syrup, leaving them for about 3 minutes so the syrup penetrates the pastries, then remove to a plate and sprinkle generously with sesame seeds. Allow to cool before serving.

Yield: 24 pastries

ALGERIAN ALMOND COOKIES

These rich almond cookies from Algeria are another popular North African dessert. They are delicious served with coffee of any kind or with Moroccan Mint Tea (see recipe, p. 222).

2   small eggs, one separated
1⅓ cups powdered sugar, plus
     extra for coating
3½ cups ground almonds

Rind of ½ lemon, grated
2   teaspoons baking powder
     Orange-flower or rose water,
     to taste

In a mixing bowl, beat 1 whole egg, 1 egg yolk, and the sugar thoroughly together, then mix in the ground almonds, lemon rind, baking powder, and orange-flower or rose water to taste. Knead well with your hands to release the oil from the almonds, and add some of the remaining egg white if necessary to make a soft, workable paste.

Using oiled hands, roll walnut-sized pieces of the almond mixture into egg-shaped balls. Cover a plate with powdered sugar and flatten the balls on the powdered sugar. Place the balls well apart on the baking sheet and bake for about 15 minutes until golden.

Yield: 30 cookies

GAZELLE'S HORNS (TCHARAK)

These popular, curved Algerian pastries are also known by their French name, *cornes de gazelles*. Variations of them can be found all over North Africa. The orange-flower water can be diluted with regular water if it smells too strong.

2	cups ground blanched almonds	1¾	cups all-purpose flour
⅓	cup caster sugar (a superfine sugar)		A pinch of salt
½	teaspoon ground cinnamon	2	tablespoons sunflower oil
⅔	to ¾ cup orange-flower water, plus 2 tablespoons		Powdered sugar for garnish

Combine the almonds, sugar, cinnamon, and 2 tablespoons of the orange-flower water, and knead to a stiff paste; set aside.

Preheat the oven to 350 degrees. Oil a baking sheet.

To make the pastry, sift the flour and salt in a mixing bowl and mix together with the oil. Stir in just enough orange-flower water to bring it together as a soft dough. Knead well until smooth and elastic. On a lightly floured surface, roll out the dough very thinly and cut into 3 by 6-inch long strips.

Break off pieces of filling about the size of a walnut and roll them into thin sausage shapes about 3 inches long with tapering ends. Place lengthwise along the edge of the strips of dough, about 1¼ inches apart.

Dampen the pastry edges with water and fold the pastry over to cover the filling. Seal the edges. Cut around the humps of filling with the point of a sharp knife and press the cut edges together to seal.

Carefully curve the pastries into horn or crescent shapes and place on the baking sheet. Bake for 20 to 25 minutes until lightly browned. Allow to cool on a wire rack then dust with powdered sugar.

Yield: 16 pastries

WALNUT "SANDWICH" CANDIES

Walnuts combined with a rose water-flavored almond mixture make a fitting and delicious end to a Tunisian meal.

¾	cup ground almonds	1	tablespoon lemon juice
1	teaspoon rose water	⅔	cup water
1	egg yolk, beaten	¾	cup sugar,
24	walnut halves		plus extra for coating

Mix the ground almonds with the rose water, then add enough egg yolk to bind the ingredients together. Use the almond mixture to fill "sandwiches" made of the walnut halves.

In a saucepan, mix the lemon juice with the water. Gently heat the sugar in this liquid, stirring until the sugar has dissolved. Raise the heat and boil until the syrup is reduced by half.

Using a slotted spoon, lower the walnuts into the syrup and coat well. Lift out and roll in sugar to coat evenly. Allow to dry overnight.

Yield: 12 candies

Glossary of African Food and Cooking Terms

Ata: The generic term for chile pepper among the Yoruba of Nigeria. *Ata funfun* resembles the jalapeño, while *ata wewe* is a tabasco-like chile. *Ata rodo* is *Capsicum chinense,* the habanero relative.

Bakolocal: A cultivated variety of chile in Ethiopia.

Barkono: The term for chile in northern Nigeria.

Berbere: The Amharic word for chile; in Ethiopia the term refers generically to both the pod and a paste made from the pods.

Bobotie: A South African curried casserole.

Bush meat: Game.

Couscous: A North African semolina grain and the dishes cooked with it.

Fatalii: The term for the chinense species in the Central Africa Republic. Extremely hot.

Felfel al har: The Arabic term for hot chile pepper in North Africa.

Gombo: Okra.

Groundnuts: Peanuts.

Guinea pepper: Thought to be of the *chinense* species, it is grown in Nigeria, Liberia, and the Ivory Coast.

Harissa: A North African chile paste.

Injera: A large Ethiopian pancake made from fermented batter. It serves as the country's bread, tablecloth, and silverware all in one.

Jollof rice: A rice dish made with meat, poultry, or fish that is popular in West Africa. It is usually highly spiced with chiles. Also spelled "wolof."

Kefta: A spicy North African meatball dish.

Kerrie: The Afrikaans (South African) term for curry.

Kima: A Kenyan stew with red chiles.

Kitfo: A raw meat dish in Ethiopia; usually beef or lamb.

Mano: The term for chile in Liberia.

Marekofana: A cultivated variety of chile in Ethiopia.

Mealie: Corn.

Pawpaw: Papaya.

Peri-Peri: See *pili-pili.*

Pili-pili: The Swahili term for the *chiltepin,* or bird's-eye pepper, in tropical Africa. Generically, all hot chile peppers in Africa.

Piri-Piri: See *pili-pili.* Also describes dishes made with this hot pepper in Mozambique and Kenya.

Pujei: The term for chile in Sierra Leone.

Pusa Jwala: A cultivated chile in Liberia.

Ras al hanout: Literally, "top of the shop;" a North African spice mixture containing up to thirty ingredients.

Sakaipilo: The term for hot chile pepper in Madagascar.

Sambal: A Malaysian chile paste exported to South Africa.

Shatta: An Arabic term for hot chile pepper.

Sosaties: South African kebabs, usually lamb.

Tabil: A spice mixture from Tunisia.

Tajine: A North African stew.

We't: Ethopian chile-laden stews of chicken, meat, fish, or vegetables. Also spelled *wa't.*

Zahtar: A spice mixture from North Africa.

Bibliography

A-As-Saqui. "Tomato and Pepper Production and Its Problems in Liberia." *Tomato and Pepper Production in the Tropics.* Edited by T.D. Griggs and B.T. McLean. Taipei, Taiwan: Asian Vegetable Research and Development Center, 1989.

Abrahams, Cass. *The Culture & Cuisine of the Cape Malays.* Welgemoed, South Africa: Metz Press, 1995.

Ayenzu, Dinah Ameley. *The Art of West African Cooking.* Garden City, NY: Doubleday & Co., 1972.

Bayley, Monica. *Black African Cook Book.* San Francisco: Determined Productions, 1977.

Chapman, Pat. *Favourite Middle Eastern Recipes.* London: Judy Piatkus Publishers, 1989.

Coetzee, Renata. *The South African Culinary Tradition.* Cape Town, South Africa: C. Struik Publishers, 1977.

Cox, Michelle. Personal correspondence with Kenyan recipes. Malindi, Kenya: January 25, 1996.

De Schlippe, Pierre. *Shifting Cultivation in Africa.* London: Routledge & Kegan Paul, 1956.

DeWitt, Dave and Nancy Gerlach. *The Whole Chile Pepper Book.* Boston: Little, Brown, 1990.

DeWitt, Dave and Arthur Pais. *A World of Curries.* Boston: Little, Brown, 1994.

DeWitt, Dave and Chuck Evans. *The Hot Sauce Bible.* Freedom, CA: The Crossing Press, 1996.

DeWitt, Dave and Nancy Gerlach. "In Hottest Africa, Part 1." *Chile Pepper* (Nov/Dec 1990): 20.

DeWitt, Dave and Nancy Gerlach. "In Hottest Africa, Part 2." *Chile Pepper* (Jan/Feb 1991): 20.

Eames, Alan D. *Secret Life of Beer.* Pownal, VT: Storey Communications, 1995.

Egerton, John. "The African Legacy." *The Great Food Almanac,* by Irena Chalmers. San Francisco: CollinsPublishers, 1994.

Erinie, I.D. "Present Status and Prospects for Increased Production of Tomato and Pepper in Northern Nigeria." *Tomato and Pepper Production in the Tropics.* Edited by T.D. Griggs and B.T. McLean. Taipei, Taiwan: Asian Vegetable Research and Development Center, 1989.

Gardner, Ann. *Karibu: Welcome to the Cooking of Kenya.* Nairobi, Kenya: Kenway Publications, 1992.

Gerber, Hilda. *Traditional Cookery of the Cape Malays.* Amsterdam/Cape Town: A.A. Balkema, 1958.

Githens, Thomas S. and Carroll E. Wood, Jr. *The Food Resources of Africa.* Philadelphia: University of Pennsylvania Press, 1943.

Govindarajan, V.S. "Capsicum—Production, Technology, Chemistry, and Quality, Part 2." *Critical Reviews in Food Science and Nutritition* 23:3 (1986): 212.

Grant, Rosamund. *Taste of Africa.* New York: Smithmark, 1995.

Green, Arlin and Susan Hunter. *Tropical Appetites: Fine Cooking and Dining in Tanzania.* Dar es Salaam, Tanzania: Gecko Publishing, 1995.

Green, Arlin and Susan Hunter. "Four Styles of Tanzanian Cooking." Unpublished ms., 1995.

Hachten, Harva. *Kitchen Safari.* New York: Atheneum, 1970.

Haffner, Dorinda. *A Taste of Africa.* Berkeley, CA: Ten Speed Press, 1993.

Haile, Y. and Y. Zewdie. "Hot Pepper and Tomato Production and Research in Ethiopia." *Tomato and Pepper Production in the Tropics.* Edited by T.D. Griggs and B.T. McLean. Taipei, Taiwan: Asian Vegetable Research and Development Center, 1989.

Halasz, Zoltan. *Hungarian Paprika Through the Ages.* Budapest: Corvina Press, 1963.

Harris, Jessica B. *Iron Pots and Wooden Spoons.* New York: Ballantine Books, 1989.

Hayward, Yvonne, ed. *A Zimbabwean Cookery Book.* Gweru, Zimbabwe: Mambo Press, 1967.

Hillman, Howard. *The Book of World Cuisines.* New York: Penguin Books, 1979.

Hilton, Richard and Leslie Richfield. *Seafood Specialties from Southern Africa's Top Restaurateurs.* Edenvale, South Africa: Hilton-Richfield, 1986.

Hudgins, Sharon. "Couscous Royale." *Chile Pepper* (Jan/Feb 1990): 30.

Hultman, Tami, ed. *The Africa News Cookbook*. New York: Penguin Books, 1986.

Irvine, F.R. *West African Crops*. London: Oxford University Press, 1969.

Isnard, Leon. *La Gastronomie Africaine*. Paris: Albin Michel, 1930.

Jordan, Clared. *List of Foods Used in Africa*. Rome: United States Foreign Agricultural Office, 1970.

Livingstone, A.D. and Helen. *Edible Plants and Animals: Unusual Foods from Aardvark to Zamia*. New York: Facts on File, 1993.

Kraus, Barbara. *The Cookbook of the United Nations*. New York: United Nations Association of the U.S.A., Inc., 1964.

Lesberg, Sandy. *The Art of African Cooking*. New York: Dell Publishing Co., 1971.

Mayat, Zuleikha, ed. *Indian Delights*. Durban, South Africa: Women's Cultural Group, 1961.

Medearis, Angela Shelf. *The African-American Kitchen*. New York: Dutton, 1994.

Members of St. Andrews Church Woman's Guild. *The Kenya Cookery Book*. Nairobi, Kenya: Kenway Publications, 1994. (Originally published in 1928).

Mendes, Helen. *The African Heritage Cookbook*. New York: The Macmillan Company, 1971.

Merriam, Barbara. "The Ubiquitous Hot Pepper." *Chile Pepper* (May/June 1995): 44.

Merson, Annette. *African Cooking*. Nashville, TN: Winston-Derek Publishers, 1987.

Mesfin, D.J. *Exotic Ethiopian Cooking*. Falls Church, VA: Ethiopian Cookbook Enterprises, 1990.

Ogilvie, Rosemary Ann. "The Back Roads of Morocco." *Chile Pepper* (Jan/Feb 1995): 15.

Ominde, Mary. *Mary Ominde's African Cookery Book*. Nairobi, Kenya: Kenway Publications, 1984.

Purseglove, J.W., et al. "Chillies: Capsicum spp." *Spices*. London and New York: Longman, 1981.

Ritter, Judith. "Madagascar in Montreal." *Chile Pepper* (Jan/Feb 1991): 32.

Rood, Betsie. *Betsie Rood's 101 Traditional South African Recipes*. Cape Town: Tafelberg Publishers, 1977.

Root, Waverly. *Food*. New York: Simon and Schuster, 1980.

Sandler, Bea. *The African Cookbook*. New York: Citadel Press, 1994.

Schwabe, Calvin W. *Unmentionable Cuisine*. Charlottesville: University Press of Virginia, 1979.

Shaxson, Annabel, Pat Dixon, and June Walker. *The Cook Book*. Zomba, Malawi: Government Printer, 1974.

Simmons, Mary Beth. "Agnes' Hoof Soup." *Chile Pepper* (May/June 1995): 45.

Simson, Sally. *The Cape of Good Cooks*. Rivonia, South Africa: William Waterman Publications, 1994.

Sokolov, Raymond. *Why We Eat What We Eat*. New York: Touchstone, 1991.

Sterling, Richard. "No Road to Zanzibar." *Chile Pepper* (July/Aug 1995): 16.

Stevenel, L. "Red Pepper, A Too Much Forgotten Therapeutic Agent Against Anorexia, Liver Congestion, and Vascular Troubles." *Bulletin Soc. Patho. Exot.* 49:5 (1956): 841–3.

Synman, Lannice. *Reflections of the South African Table*. Hout Bay, South Africa: S&S Publishers, 1996.

Synman, Lannice and Anne Klarie. *New Free From the Sea: The South African Seafood Cookbook*. Cape Town, South Africa: Struik Publishers, Ltd., 1994.

Tannahill, Reay. *Food in History*. New York: Crown Publishers, 1988.

Toussaint-Samat, Maguelonne. *History of Food*. Cambridge, MA: Blackwell Publishers, 1992.

van der Post, Laurens. *African Cooking*. New York: Time-Life Books, 1970.

van der Post, Laurens. *First Catch Your Eland*. New York: William Morrow, 1978.

Walden, Hilaire. *North African Cooking*. Edison, NJ: Chartwell Books, Inc., 1995.

Warren, D. Michael and Jennifer Pinkston. "Indigenous African Resource Management of a Tropical Rain Forest Ecosystem: A Case Study of the Yoruba of Ara, Nigeria." Ames, IA: Center for Indigenous Knowledge for Agriculture and Rural Development, 1995.

Warren, D. Michael and Mary, Michael McNulty, and Jason Walsmith. "The Pepper Paradise of Ara, Nigeria." Ames, IA: Center for Indigenous Knowledge for Agriculture and Rural Development, 1995.

Wells, Troth. *The World in Your Kitchen*. Freedom, CA: The Crossing Press, 1993.

Wells, Troth. *The Global Kitchen*. Freedom, CA: The Crossing Press, 1995.

Williams, Faldela. *The Cape Malay Cookbook*. Cape Town, South Africa: C. Struik Publishers, 1988.

Wilson, Ellen Gibson. *A West African Cookbook*. New York: M. Evans & Co., 1971.

Wolfert, Paula. *Couscous and Other Good Food from Morocco*. New York: Perennial Library, 1987.

Zehnder, Nick. "Bunny Chow." *Chile Pepper* (May/June 1995): 46.

Mail-Order Sources

Hundreds of companies now carry chile pepper products; it is impossible to list them all here. The companies below carry a wide variety of ingredients and products mentioned in the recipes in this book.

Brother Bru Bru's
P.O. Box 2964
Venice, CA 90291
(310) 396-9033

African hot sauces.

Chile Today, Hot Tamale
919 Highway 33, Suite 47
Freehold, NJ 07728
(800) 468-7377

Habanero hot sauces and other products.

Caribbean Food Products
1936 N. Second Avenue
Jacksonville Beach, FL 32250
(904) 246-0149

Trinidadian Congo pepper sauces.

Coyote Cocina
1364 Rufina Circle, #1
Santa Fe, NM 87501
(800) 866-HOWL

Hot sauces and other chile products.

Dat'l Do It
P.O. Box 4019
St. Augustine, FL 32084
(800) HOT-DATL

Grower of fresh Datil peppers; manufacturer of Datil pepper products. Datil pepper seeds.

Dean and DeLuca
Mail Order Department
560 Broadway
New York, NY 10012
(212) 431-1691

Exotic herbs and spices from around the world.

Enchanted Seeds
P.O. Box 6087
Las Cruces, NM 88006
(505) 233-3033

Habanero and other exotic chile seeds.

Frieda's, Inc.
P.O. Box 584888
Los Angeles, CA 90058
(800) 421-9477

Shipper of fresh and dried habaneros, other chiles, and exotic produce.

Gil's Gourmet Gallery
577 Ortiz Avenue
Sand City, CA 93955
(800) 438-7480

Habanero hot sauces and other products.

Hot Sauce Harry's
The Dallas Farmer's Market
3422 Flair Drive
Dallas, TX 75229
(214) 902-8552

A large collection of hot sauces.

Le Saucier
Faneuil Hall Marketplace
Boston, MA 02109
(617) 227-9649

Sauces and condiments from all over the world.

Melissa's World Variety Produce
P.O. Box 21127
Los Angeles, CA 90021
(800) 468-7111

Shipper of fresh, dried, and pickled chiles and other specialty produce.

Mo Hotta, Mo Betta
P.O. Box 4136
San Luis Obispo, CA 93403
(800) 462-3220

A wide collection of chile products.

Old Southwest Trading Company
P.O. Box 7545
Albuquerque, NM 87194
(505) 836-0168

New Mexican and Mexican chiles, sauces and salsas, Southwest gifts.

Pendery's
1221 Manufacturing
Dallas, TX 75207
(800) 533-1870

Dried chiles, spices, and other chile products.

Perk's Peri Peri
20 H Putnam Green
Greenwich, CT 06831
(203) 532-9454.

African hot sauces.

Santa Fe School of Cooking
116 W. San Francisco Street
Santa Fe, NM 87501
(505) 983-4511

Chile seeds, dried and pickled pods, and other hot and spicy products.

Shepherd's Garden Seeds
30 Irene Street
Torrington, CT 06790
(860) 482-3638

Chile pepper and exotic
vegetable seeds.

Index